POSTCARDS
FROM LIVERPOOL

Beatles Moments & Memories

MARK BRICKLEY

CONTENTS

THE CAVERN CLUB: AUGUST 3, 1963

Every inch of space was taken in the subterranean nightclub. The girls in the front row swayed to the music. Vocalists John Lennon and Paul McCartney were on fire and George Harrison's lead guitar roared. The crowd screamed as drummer Ringo Starr struck the downbeat to the Beatles No.1 UK Hit "Please Please Me."

As the last chord echoed, Liverpool's most famous band was spirited to a waiting car. Hundreds of fans unable to get tickets remained queued up out front. After 292 appearances this would be the Beatles last Cavern Club show. Now everyone in Britain clamored to hear them. Soon the whole world would be listening.

The Cavern Club, Liverpool 2015

PREFACE

If you shake a bottle of pop – and flip the top – it explodes. That's what happened to the Beatles. It felt like they arrived from another universe, with crystalline harmonies and a flawless, pristine sound that was beyond compare. From 1962-70 the Beatles recorded melodies that teens and adults yearned to hear. Those songs continue to spark, glow and move together like parallel lines. The passage of time has not diminished the power and significance of the Beatles music.

The Beatles' musicianship and cohesiveness defined their success and legacy. Band members viewed themselves as professionals and worked hard to perfect their craft as musicians and singers. Their songs featured unexpected chord changes and startling phrasing, driven by deep vocal emotion. They were also a focused, close knit group. At their mid-sixties peak the Beatles' inner circle consisted of just five key people: personal manager Brian Epstein, press officer Derek Taylor, publicist Tony Barrow, road manager Neil Aspinall and personal assistant/roadie Mal Evans.

The idea for *Postcards From Liverpool* came from my 2010 article titled *The Beatles First Record*, which was published on website *Noozhawk.com*. Over the next two years I regularly featured the Beatles in my *Coastal View News* music columns. My editor joked that she was going to change the column's name from the *Music Beat* to the *Beatles Beat*. I got her drift but I continued to explore the band's music on my own time.

Official Beatles biographer Hunter Davis stated he wished he'd spent more time directly observing how Lennon & McCartney wrote their songs. Exploring how the Beatles created their sound and which artists influenced them were the roots of my research. I deconstructed the Beatles layered vocals, studied their songwriting techniques and explored their studio innovations. After reading Beatles biographies by George Martin, Mark Lewisohn, Barry Miles, Geoff Emrick and others, I traveled to see Beatles exhibits at Cleveland's Rock Hall and Seattle's EMP museum. At Sir Ringo Starr's Los Angles Grammy Museum press conference I asked the famed drummer about his view of the Beatles legacy. After photographing Sir Paul McCartney outside Capitol Records, I began to see a book emerging.

My goal was to focus on the Beatles musical magic rather than mirror the band's flaws. *Postcards From Liverpool* takes an indirect route to explore the Beatles mosaic; from the back-story of how the band struggled to record their original music, to tracking their musical influences from Detroit's

Motown sound to George Harrison's immersion in Indian music and religion. To better understand the Beatles vision, I traced their footsteps through London to Liverpool, visiting both George Harrison's modest childhood flat in Arnold Grove and Sir Ringo Starr's early haunts in Dingle's Admiral Grove. I also booked docent led British National Trust tours of Sir Paul McCartney's and John Lennon's teenage homes and stood inside Lennon's front entryway where he and Paul practiced their early harmonies. My side trips included the updated Beatles *Cirque du Soleil "Love"* show in Las Vegas and experiencing Lennon's memorial in NYC's Central Park. Each tour, event and exhibition confirmed the unbreakable bond that music fans still have with the famed Liverpool quartet.

Postcards From Liverpool's 2017 publication led to unexpected Beatles experiences which I've spotlighted in the 2019 edition. Its two dozen new photographs and four additional chapters include my meet-up with a former Beatle at the San Diego Beatles Fair and insights from the 2018 International White Album Symposium held at New Jersey's Monmouth University. I also tell the story of an unlikely English pop singer who kept two of the Beatles greatest singles from reaching the top of the British charts. Chapter *Here, There & Everything Beatles* includes a primer on how to collect 60's vinyl records, listings of the major Beatles festivals, touring international Beatles sites and much more.

If wandering along a crooked path can open hidden vistas, I hope this updated ramble will give you new insight into the Beatles craft and magic. Maybe we will meet again somewhere down their winding road, under a marmalade sky.

Cheers from,
MARK BRICKLEY
April 2019

BACKSTORIES

"Before the Beatles, music was stamped out like cookies. It was hopeless in England and on the BBC. The Beatles were a breath of fresh air that never stopped blowing."
— *Jackie Lomax, lead singer/bassist of 1960s Liverpool band, The Undertakers*

Popular music has been shaped like layers of geologic strata and the Beatles helped form its core. The Beatles' original Parlophone albums are this book's bedrock. John, Paul, George and Ringo's songs are recognized around the world, but how they found their sound and who influenced them–that is more obscure. The following eight backstories explore the band's foundation, innovations and experimentation. Its final story offers a panorama of the Beatles' 1968 journey to Rishikesh, India.

JOHN'S WOOD

BEATLES COFFEE SHOP

OFFICIAL BEATLE
MERCHANDISE

FOOD AND DRIN

www.BeatlesCoffeeSh

**Beatles Shop at St. John's Wood
Tube station, London 2015**

BEGINNINGS

The Beatles rise to fame is one of pop music's most improbable stories. They were a musical tsunami. In April 1964, eighteen months after the release of their first UK single, the Beatles occupied the top five spots on the American Billboard Hot 100 chart. It's never happened since. By May 1965, they had sold one hundred million records. Not bad for the twenty-something sons of four working class Liverpool families.

Persistence may be creativity's most under-appreciated component. To American audiences, the Beatles' staggering celebrity appeared sudden and overwhelming. In truth, their "lightning success" was the result of six years of practice and consistent performance. Before their first Parlophone recording session, the band had played over 800 live shows in Northern England, Scotland and Germany.

They began in 1956 as a skiffle group playing folk, blues and American pop hits on second-hand instruments. Skiffle was British slang for make-shift. By 1958 John Lennon's band, The Quarrymen, had downsized to a trio. The band would have nine name changes. Lennon, McCartney and Harrison called themselves Johnny and the Moondogs when they performed at local talent shows and Liverpool social clubs.

When Ringo Starr first heard Lennon's group play in early 1960, he remembers they were still putting their material together and weren't much of a band. Liverpool art student Stuart Sutcliff became the group's bassist in late December 1959. Their live act began to gel when they were chosen to back Liverpool ballad singer Johnny Gentle on a seven-date tour of Scotland (May 20–28, 1960). After playing Gentle's covers of Elvis, Rickey Nelson and Peggy Lee, the newly-named Silver Beetles (with Tommy Moore on drums), cut loose with their own set. Their songs included "Twist and Shout," "Tuti Fruti," and originals "Hello Little Girl" and "The One After 909." George Harrison later remarked that the Scotland tour gave them hope of 'making it' someday.

The fabled act's big break wasn't a glitzy gig or being discovered by a London record company. It was an August 1960 contract to play in Hamburg, Germany's seamy nightclubs. Their four-month residency changed everything. It was their rock 'n' roll apprenticeship. While crossing the English Channel by car ferry, they dropped "Silver" from their name and became The Beatles.

In Hamburg, the Beatles tried everything to entertain their excited German audiences, and their wild performances drew big crowds. John Lennon belted out lyrics lying flat on his back and once sang with a toilet seat around his neck. Propelled by drummer Pete Best's steady rhythm, the group's improvised guitar solos went on forever.

Beatles name changes: The Blackjacks: 1956 (Lennon's shortlived first band), *The Quarrymen: 1956, Johnny and the Moondogs: 1958, Nerk Twins (Lennon & McCartney's one-off 1960 show) and later in 1960 – five names: The Beatals, The Silver Beetles, Silver Beats, The Silver Beatles and finally, The Beatles.*

Soundscape

The Beatles' sound was built around vocals but driven by instrumental prowess. Lennon's chords growled, McCartney's bass bounced, Harrison's riffs rocked and Starr's sticks snapped. Nothing was held back. On early '60s British TV and radio, the band played dozens of covers and originals filled with complex chords and unusual rhythm patterns.

Lennon said they didn't use echo or reverb to cover their chord changes the way other British groups did. They exuded musical confidence, rarely looking at their guitar fretboards. The Beatles' guitarists also played keyboard in their live shows. The organ, piano and mellotron would be featured instruments on future records.

Despite their compelling performance skills, none of the Beatles could read music or transcribe the original songs they wrote. Parlophone producer George Martin said McCartney began composition lessons but soon dropped them. Each member of the group was primarily self-taught. Before the onset of Beatlemania, no one in the band had taken guitar or keyboard lessons or received formal music instruction. As an eleven-year-old, McCartney once auditioned to sing in the Liverpool Cathedral choir but was turned down.

In *The Beatles Anthology*, George Harrison said he believed an unknown hand was guiding the band forward. He commented that he never felt anxious about the group's future and always believed they would become recording artists. Those dreams would soon become their destiny.

THE FIRST RECORD

In September 1962, the Beatles faced a decision that would transform the future of popular music.

The band had come home after playing forty-eight new dates in Hamburg, Germany, but their appearances were far from glamorous. The group played non-stop shows at the Star Club located in the city's kinky, red-light district. They had accepted their third German residency (April 12–May 31, 1962) after a disappointing audition with London's Decca Records.

Their manager, Brian Epstein, had booked the Decca demo session for January 1, 1962. They drove from Liverpool to London but got lost in bad weather, arriving late on New Year's Eve in a van packed with amplifiers and instruments. Later that morning they recorded twelve cover songs and three originals picked by Epstein. Decca Records wasn't impressed and instead signed East London band *Brian Poole and the Tremelos.*

Critics have second guessed Epstein's Decca set list, but it's more likely the Beatles sound hadn't yet crystallized. Only two of the covers and none of the originals they played that day would appear on a future Beatles Parlophone or Capitol Records album.

Liverpool

Local fans were amazed by the Beatles bold, new, rocking style. Their full-tilt Liverpool shows included numbers by Chuck Berry and Buddy Holly. McCartney's original "I Saw Her Standing There" featured Little Richard's frenzied falsetto vocal style. The only early film footage of the Beatles at the Cavern Club is dated August 22, 1962. They're playing the shaking R&B cover song "Some Other Guy," which was part of their regular set. Their riffs are tight, and their vocals shine.

The short Cavern Club film also shows how manager Epstein had begun to transform the Beatles stage appearance. Their "Teddy Boy" leather gear was gone, replaced by black slacks, skinny ties and matching sweater vests. They no longer smoked or ate sandwiches on stage, and each song ended in a choreographed bow. Epstein didn't invent the group's shaggy haircut. The band copied the combed-down, moptop look from Hamburg's art students.

Rhythm guitarist John Lennon had turned twenty-one and original drummer Pete Best was twenty years old. Lead guitarist George Harrison was nineteen. Paul McCartney (twenty) had become the group's bass player by default. Bassist Stuart Sutcliff had fallen in love and decided to remain in Hamburg. His short engagement to photographer Astrid Kirchherr would end tragically with Sutcliff dying of a brain aneurysm.

While they were playing in Germany, Epstein searched for another record deal. None of London's major labels had expressed interest. He was repeatedly turned down by Phillips, Columbia, Pye and Oriole Records, but his persistence finally paid off. Through his Liverpool record store connections he was introduced to producer George Martin, the head of EMI's (Electronic Musical Industries) Parlophone Records.

Martin was scouting new talent, hoping to supplement the labels' classical and comedy releases. He offered Epstein EMI's standard contract, contingent on the outcome of the band's demo session. The Beatles were one of several acts he was auditioning. Epstein immediately telegraphed the good news to the group in Germany.

Artist Test

In 1962, few British bands performed original songs. Most played covers of American rock or blues records. The Beatles' decision to feature their own songs was driven by their growing popularity. Their skill level had skyrocketed after playing marathon sessions in Germany. The Beatles had become Liverpool's headline band, surpassing The Big Three, The Undertakers, The Mojos and The Four Jays.

In multi-act shows, the headliner had to wait its turn to perform. Sometimes there were six or seven groups on the marquee. Sitting backstage, they often heard half their set list being played. Lennon and McCartney began to feature their own material to stand out. "Love Me Do" was written by McCartney in his mid-teens with Lennon contributing the song's bridge and harmonica solo.

The band's first London EMI recording session was set for June 6, 1962. Members rehearsed four originals, including a slow-moving version of "Please Please Me." George Martin later said the group's vocals were promising, but he wasn't overly impressed with their arrangements. The Beatles' initial recordings were overseen by assistant producer Ron Richards. He guided the band through originals "Ask Me Why" and "P.S. I Love You," but the group's amplifiers produced excessive static and background noise. They had to be jerry-rigged to continue recording. During the taping of "Love Me Do," Richards called Martin back to the studio.

McCartney revealed that the "Love Me Do" harmony, set against a syncopated beat, was difficult to master. The Beatles were playing the blues. Lennon's lips were numb from repeating the song's soulful harmonica solo. Martin invited the group to listen to the playback but was blunt about their poor equipment and spotty microphone technique.

Some have speculated that the band's spontaneity and wit sealed its recording deal. Standing in the control room, Martin asked if there was anything band members disagreed with or didn't like. Harrison spoke up first. "Well, for one thing, we don't like your tie," he deadpanned. Then the Beatles unleashed a barrage of Liverpool-style jibes, jokes and pokes. Martin and Richards reportedly laughed until tears ran down their cheeks.

Royalties

Martin's decision to sign the Beatles' contract created little risk for EMI. Single 45 rpm records sold for about a dollar in 1962, and Parlophone's contract paid only one pence for each one sold. The Beatles had to split that penny four ways. With Epstein taking 25 percent off the top, the group was left with fish-and-chips change.

The band agreed to a five-year deal to run from 1962–1967. Besides the penny-pinching first year guarantee, it included four option years at EMI's discretion, with royalty increases of one farthing (1/4 penny) up to 2 pence (2 pennies) in the fifth year.

During 1958 and 1959, the Beatles only made a few pounds each for their Liverpool gigs. The British pound equalled about $2.80 US. In 1960, Paul McCartney was allowed to travel and perform in Hamburg, Germany because he was offered a higher weekly salary than his father made. Each band member was paid fifteen pounds per week (about $42 US).

When Beatlemania gripped Britain in 1963, the group's fee climbed to 500 pounds per concert (about $1,400 US dollars). They were also able to renegotiate their Parlophone Records royalties at a substantially higher rate. On their 1964 American tour, the Beatles would be paid $150,000.00 (US) for a thirty-two minute, thirteen-song show in Kansas City, Missouri.

Drummed Out

The Beatles returned to Liverpool and resumed their busy performance schedule. Epstein had them working both noon and evening sets. After reviewing the first EMI recordings, Martin sent word to Epstein that he would have to use a studio drummer. He was blunt, stating that percussionist Pete Best couldn't play a steady beat pattern.

Martin wanted the Beatles' first record to be a sure-fire hit and thought he'd found the perfect single. The up-tempo tune "How Do You Do It?" was written by twenty-two-year-old Londoner Mitch Murray. Martin sent Epstein the song's demo and asked the Beatles to learn it. Lennon and McCartney panned the song's predictable melody and sugary lyrics but agreed to rehearse it.

The immediate concern was their drummer. He had become a liability well before their producer's edict. They had hired Best under pressure two years earlier, just before their first Hamburg gig. He was popular with female fans but the group had always wanted to find a better musician. As the band began to stretch its musical boundaries, Best's playing didn't evolve. He stuck with his on-the-beat, bass drum-driven rhythms. Now he had become a barrier to a record deal. It's likely the band viewed the problem as an opportunity.

Enter Ringo

The band wanted Northern England's best drummer. His name was Ringo Starr. Ringo's sticks powered Merseybeat band Rory Storm and the Hurricanes. They sometimes shared the stage with the Beatles in Hamburg, and Starr often hung out with his Liverpool mates.

Ringo had a nightly turn in the Hurricanes act called "Starr Time." He sang lead on covers "Alley Oop," "Boys" and the catchy Sherman Brothers tune, "You're Sixteen." His head-shaking vocals made him a compelling entertainer. Starr's reprise of "Sixteen" would become a No.1 Billboard Hit in 1973.

The decision to fire Pete Best was unanimous, but the band left the job to Epstein. The remaining members feared a fight would ensue if they were present. Epstein couldn't move until Starr agreed to leave his current group. Ringo had turned down several other offers. Liverpool band Kingsize Taylor & The Dominos wanted him to join their act in Germany. Gerry and the Pacemakers asked Starr to become their bassist even though he had never played the instrument. The Beatles offered Ringo five more pounds per week, but the real lure was news of their recording contract.

The twenty-two-year-old drummer gave Rory Storm three days' notice. On August 12, 1962, Ringo shaved his beard and became a Beatle. Lennon said he could keep his "sidebars." Two days later, Best was summoned to Epstein's office. Being direct but cautious, Epstein told Best the band had voted him out, but offered to put him in another group that he managed.

Lennon, McCartney and Harrison later said they never doubted firing Best but regretted not being more involved. Word soon spread to the Cavern Club about Best's sacking, and Harrison was later head-butted by an angry fan. His black eye is visible in photographs taken during the band's following EMI recording session.

The Single

The Beatles arrived at London's EMI studios on September 4, 1962, to record their first double-sided single record. This time Epstein flew them in from Liverpool. They rehearsed six songs, but only Murray's "How Do You

Do It?" and Lennon and McCartney's "Love Me Do" were scheduled for the evening recording session.

The rhythm and vocal track for "Love Me Do" required multiple takes to complete because of its unusual arrangement. The song's bass line and acoustic guitar are supported by a snare and double-kicked bass drum. Ringo found the beat, but George Martin was critical, saying Starr couldn't play a drum roll. Over dinner band members pressed Martin to consider their original material. They wanted to release something new and different and felt their Liverpool reputation was at stake. He rebuffed them, stating that their songs weren't hit material.

The band was unaware that EMI's publisher Ardmore & Beechwood was unhappy with Martin's plan. Ardmore & Beechwood represented the Beatles copyright but hadn't secured the publishing rights to Murray's "How Do You Do It?" The publisher didn't want one of "their" songs on the record's B side. Complicating matters was songwriter Murray's dismay with the Beatles' musical arrangement. He also refused to have his song placed on the B side of any record.

With his hit-making strategy in disarray, producer Martin was forced to concede. Despite his misgivings, he reluctantly agreed to let "Love Me Do" become the A side of their first 45 rpm single with another Beatles original, "P.S. I Love You," on the flip side. Still dissatisfied with "Love Me Do's" rhythm track, Martin scheduled another recording session.

Final Mix

When the band arrived at EMI studios on September 11, 1962, a drum kit had already been set up. Parlophone staff had been directed to book studio drummer Andy White for the session. Ringo was stunned. He had just become the group's new drummer and was being replaced on its first single. The decision wouldn't be altered. Manager Epstein was back in Liverpool, and George Martin was away from the studio on business. All Ringo could do that day was play tambourine and maracas. Although Martin later praised his drumming, Starr always remembered the slight.

Interview with British Drummer Andy White

In 2012, I spoke by phone with eighty-one-year-old drummer Andy White. In addition to his most famous job, White played on several of Herman's Hermits top singles and Tom Jones' No. 1 UK Hit "It's Not Unusual." White recounted his 1962 Beatles recording session.

***

Andy White: The call from EMI seemed routine. I'd worked at EMI/Abbey Road regularly. I didn't know I would be playing with the Beatles until I set up my drums that morning. My wife was from the North, but I hadn't heard of them.

Q: What happened when you met the Beatles that day?

White: I said hello to Ringo and George, but it was mostly business. I chatted with the songwriters (Lennon and

McCartney) about the music. We recorded several songs in three hours, but there were multiple takes because we stopped and started.

Q: What do you remember about the group's music?

White: The Beatles' creativity was apparent. Their material was original, which was fresh. They didn't use any written music. I cottoned the drum part to "Love Me Do" to follow Paul's bass line.

Q: What happened after the session?

White: I never talked with any of the Beatles after the session ended. For twenty years they didn't publicize my playing on "Love Me Do" and "P.S. I Love You." The band didn't want that fact to come out.

For his drumming that day, White received union wages of less than six pounds, about $16 US. Not much take-home pay, but memories lasting a lifetime.

The Release

"Love Me Do" had now been recorded with three different drummers: Pete Best on June 6, Ringo Starr on September 4 and Andy White on September 11. When the 45 rpm record was released on October 5, 1962, Ringo's drumming had been chosen. Starr played tambourine on White's version of "Love Me Do" and there was no tambourine on the new record.

White's bongo playing was featured on the record's B side, "P.S. I Love You," with Starr on maracas. (Note: A cover of "Love Me Do" with Starr singing lead was included on Ringo's eleventh post-Beatles 1998 album, *Vertical Man*.)

The Beatles appeared on a live British radio broadcast just after the record's initial launch. Listening fifty years later, you can feel the crowd's excitement. The announcer attempts to introduce the band, but his voice is immediately overwhelmed by screaming fans. England's teen music scene was vibrant and volatile, and the Beatles were about to make it explode.

Response to "Love Me Do" was strong in Liverpool, and sales were robust throughout the North. With little publicity from EMI and the band's decision to honor their final Hamburg nightclub contract, the single still reached #17 on the British charts.

In 1963 George Martin's handpicked song "How Do You Do it?" became a No. 1 UK Hit for Merseybeat group Gerry and the Pacemakers. Managed by Epstein, the Pacemakers reportedly used the Beatles' demo as their template. When "Love Me Do" was released in America in 1964, it climbed to the top of the Billboard Hot 100 chart.

Destiny

The Beatles changed the direction of popular music by challenging the use of outside songwriters. Their ambition to record original music fueled their success, but their destiny was forged by opportunities with uncertain outcomes.

Stuart Sutcliffe's decision to remain in Germany compelled Paul McCartney to pick up the bass guitar. Replacing drummer Pete Best with Ringo Starr cemented the band's chemistry. It propelled Lennon's, McCartney's and Harrison's songwriting success.

Hiring tenacious manager Brian Epstein led to producer George Martin. Epstein changed the group's performance style but never interfered with their music. Martin helped translate the band's melodic genius into unparalleled musical creations.

In just eight years the Beatles recorded and released 219 original songs. Their twelve top-selling British studio albums (plus EP Magical Mystery Tour) and twenty American No.1 Billboard Hit singles remain the "gold standard" of popular music.

It all began in Liverpool, in '62, with "Love Me Do."

PARALLEL THIRDS

Early '60s British pop bands were often formed around a single singer. The Beatles were different: they had two lead vocalists. When producer Martin first heard them sing at the Cavern Club he remembered their unusual harmonies. Vocal harmony is formed by singing separate but simultaneous notes at specific intervals. Lennon and McCartney sang melody and harmony in parallel thirds.

The duo formed its harmonies by singing one-third lower or higher against the melody line. Lennon often sang the lower lead with McCartney reaching the high notes. Lennon's rocking rumble mixed perfectly with McCartney's smooth tenor. Adding Harrison's mid-range voice completed the band's tri-part blend. Harrison sometimes sang a middle harmony line or doubled the melody.

The Beatles were influenced by '50s vocal duo The Everly Brothers, who sang together in close harmony. The Beatles varied the Everly template by adding R&B-style backing vocals and alternating harmony within the song. The use of blended melody and harmony gave their originals an unpredictable sparkle.

On February 16, 1964, the Beatles performed six songs, including the ballad "This Boy," on CBS television's *The Ed Sullivan Show*. It was their second appearance on his Sunday evening variety program. The concert was broadcast live from

Miami Beach's elegant Deville Hotel. Its setting had the feel of an intimate concert rather than a nationwide telecast. Lennon, McCartney and Harrison's voices shifted against major and minor chords. Their harmonies were split into perfect thirds. It's a stunning example of the Beatles' multi-part vocal style.

The unusual 12/8 time signature of "This Boy" moves along like a Thames River tributary. The song was influenced by Smokey Robinson and the Miracles' 1961 release "I've Been Good To You" and Bobby Freeman's single "You Don't Understand Me." All three songs have Doo-Wop roots and similar chord progressions.

In "This Boy," Harrison triple strums his Gretch electric to McCartney's ebbing bass line. As the ballad builds, Lennon's voice becomes anguished and desperate. Harrison answers with a stunning sixth chord. Suddenly the bridge drops and dissolves into the song's trailing melody. It's a Beatles harmonic masterpiece.

EMI/Abbey Road Studios, London, 2015

FOUR-MAN BAND

John Lennon stretched his voice beyond its breaking point. His vocals were urgent, intense and pitch perfect. Every note mattered to him. There was never hesitation in Lennon's delivery. Listeners heard every vowel and consonant. It was a voice you remembered. Lennon's vocals jump out of the speakers and knock you down. You can't escape their velocity and impact.

He sang lead on many early Beatles hits, including "She Loves You," "You Can't Do That" and "Twist and Shout." Lennon's voice dominated the band's third Parlophone LP, *A Hard Day's Night*. He wrote most of its songs, and ten of the twelve tracks feature his lead vocal. It was the first Beatles' album to include all originals.

Lennon's most piercing compositions were lyrical windows, reflections of his inner life. Songs "Help" and "I'm a Loser" revealed the edges of his personality. "Strawberry Fields Forever" and "I'm Only Sleeping" featured shifting chord shapes and mystic, wandering melodies. Lennon also penned poignant love songs. *The White Album*'s "Julia" was his only Beatles solo vocal and instrumental recording. It's a poetic, flowing tribute to his mother Julia with lyric references to wife Yoko Ono.

Given the Beatles' runaway success, it's ironic that Lennon was always nervous about the sound of his voice. He once asked George Martin if he could feed his vocals directly into the recording console. Martin joked that could only happen if the mic cord was plugged into his throat.

Lennon said he wanted his vocals on "Tomorrow Never Knows" to sound like he was singing from a distant mountain top. Audio engineers modulated Lennon's voice giving it an echo chamber timber by channeling its signal through a spinning Leslie speaker, which was often matched with the Hammond B3 organ. EMI engineer Geoff Emrick re-wired the Leslie's speaker input and attached a vocal mic for Lennon to use. Later George Harrison used a similar effect for his guitar work on songs "Lucy In The Sky With Diamonds" and "You Never Give Me Your Money."

A young waitress in Camarillo, CA had Lennon's likeness tattooed on her calf. She said "He's my musical inspiration."

Hard Rhythm

When he started his first band, Lennon only knew a few misshapen banjo chords. McCartney remembers John's guitar was missing a string. In *The Beatles Anthology*, Lennon describes himself as a "primitive musician." He never claimed to be a great technical player but said he could make the guitar sing.

Lennon usually played a black electric Rickenbacker six-string. His riffs jump off the vinyl on the up-tempo song "The Ballad of John & Yoko." Only Lennon and McCartney played on the 1968 single, because Starr was on holiday and Harrison was in India. We hear Lennon's lead voice and vibrant electric slide guitar, while McCartney sings harmony and plays drums and bass.

Family friends showed Lennon basic harmonica fingerings, and later, he bummed playing tips from touring American blues legend Delbert McClinton. Early in his career, McClinton played harp behind blues legends Lightnin' Hopkins, Howlin' Wolf and Jimmy Reed. He met Lennon in Liverpool in 1962 while touring with Bruce Channel. The American rocker's song "Hey Baby" was a No. 1 Hit in both the US and UK. Lennon's harmonica riffs are heard on just twelve Beatles singles and album tracks including "Love Me Do," "Please Please Me," "From Me To You," "I'm A Loser" and "Rocky Raccoon."

Bass Lines

Producer Martin realized the Beatles' market potential after listening to McCartney sing on the Decca demos. Paul's vocals glowed and his phrasing seemed effortless. He jumped octaves with ease and new melodies appeared in his dreams.

McCartney is known for composing expressive ballads including "Yesterday," "I Will" and "Blackbird," but he's also a ferocious singer. The band's live shows featured his raucous version of Little Richard's "Long Tall Sally" and raw original "I Saw Her Standing There." McCartney's vocals would later rock the *White Album*'s "Birthday" and "Helter Skelter." In songs "I'm Down" and "Let It Be" his voice builds, burns, and explodes.

George Martin complimented McCartney's growing keyboard skills, revealing that McCartney took both voice and piano lessons after the band began recording. An example of McCartney's musicality is revealed on his demo of the song "Fool on the Hill." The solo piano and vocal recording is available on Apple Records' *Anthology 2*.

In 1957, Lennon asked McCartney to join The Quarrymen because of his guitar skills. He also knew all the lyrics to Gene Vincent's "Be-Bop-A-Lula" and played Eddie Cochran's "Twenty Flight Rock" note-for-note. McCartney likely learned guitar on his own, but received the most in-family music instruction of the Beatles.

His father was a semi-professional trumpet player and 'pick-up' pianist who performed with Liverpool's Jimmy Mac Jazz Band. Jim McCartney played songs like 1932's "I'll Build A Stairway to Paradise." The Tin Pan Alley standard has the feel of Beatles' song "When I'm Sixty- Four." Jim likely taught his son basic piano chords, trumpet fingerings and vocal harmony.

Because he's left-handed, McCartney played both bass and electric guitars upside down until he could afford left-oriented instruments. Paul bought his first violin-shaped Hofner bass in Liverpool when he returned from Hamburg in 1960 and later used a Rickenbacker electric bass on the band's studio albums.

He remains one of rock's most accomplished and melodic bassists, shaping bass lines like a lead guitarist. McCartney also became a proficient drummer and played percussion on Beatles' tracks "Dear Prudence" and rocker "Back in the USSR" after Ringo Starr temporarily left the group in 1968.

Bending Notes

In the beginning he rarely sang. George Harrison was fourteen when he was invited to play guitar in The Quarrymen. His staccato riffs and bright chord combinations brought flash and flair to their early repertoire.

The Beatles' all-night gigs in Hamburg gave Harrison the freedom to expand his singing role. He took the lead on Chuck Berry's "Roll Over Beethoven" and became the middle voice in the band's layered harmonies. Harrison's vocals were first heard on 1963's *Please Please Me* album. On song "Chains," Harrison's phrasing is clear and confident. Listeners will also notice his strong Liverpool accent on the ballad "Do You Want To Know A Secret."

Harrison developed an extraordinary musical vocabulary and was the band's most dedicated guitarist. He was an encyclopedia of chords. Legend has it that he first played guitar for Lennon and McCartney on the top of a Penny Lane double-decker bus. The actual tryout happened at a Liverpool basement nightclub called The Morgue. Harrison's audition included his rendition of "Guitar Boogie," a rocking instrumental shuffle written by Arthur Smith in 1945.

His first guitar was a Hofner acoustic he electrified by screwing a magnetic pickup into the sound hole. Harrison played a variety of electric guitars on Beatles' recordings including the twelve-string Rickenbacker he was given in 1964 and a Fender Stratocaster he used during the making of *Rubber Soul*.

In 2012, several of Harrison's guitars were exhibited at the Los Angeles Grammy Museum, including his black Gretsch Duo Jet and a psychedelically painted Fender. Harrison sang lead on all of his Beatles originals. His songwriting credits include "Don't Bother Me," "I Need You," "Taxman," "Here Comes The Sun" and "Something." Harrison's "If I Needed Someone" was the only original he performed on the band's worldwide tours. His passion for Indian music would transform the band's creative direction.

Back Beat

Ringo Starr's wild 1964 rendition of "I Wanna Be Your Man" was captured on film at the Washington Coliseum. Starr's sticks fly and his hair shakes to the beat. Ringo throws his whole body into the lyrics and his voice booms with excitement.

Starr was seventeen when the skiffle craze hit Liverpool. His stepfather bought him a second-hand drum kit in 1957. Starr performed in Eddie Clayton's Skiffle Group, Dark Town Skiffle and Al Caldwell's Texans. In 1959, the Texans' lead singer Caldwell changed his stage name to Rory Storm. With Starr on drums, Rory Storm and the Hurricanes became one of Liverpool's top rock bands. Ringo played a range of beats, from blues to syncopated swing. His steady rhythms were always in sync with the band's singer. He became known as a drummer who could handle shifting time signatures.

Because Starr was also left-handed, his drum fills (snare to tom-tom to cymbals) and beat patterns had unusual accents. Ringo liked to muffle the snap of his snare with a pack of cigarettes or a towel. He said he couldn't play the same drum sequence twice, but was acknowledged as the North's top "in-the-pocket" rhythmist. Starr's creative drumming and solo work are showcased in Beatles songs "Rain" and "Birthday." Lennon's requiem "In My Life" is propelled by Ringo's off-the-beat rhythm. His bright tambourine and tight fills spark the band's No.1 Hit "Ticket to Ride."

Ringo's vocals would be featured on almost every Beatles album, from country cover "Act Naturally" to sing-along "Yellow Submarine." While he had a limited range (about five notes), Lennon and McCartney wrote songs that matched his vocal breadth. Ringo's tracks offered listeners a diversion from the band's dominant singers. Starr's voice was strong and direct, an extension of his engaging personality.

It was Lennon's idea to write a call-and-response song for Ringo to sing on the *Sgt. Pepper's Lonely Hearts Club* album. Starr wasn't sure he could stretch his voice high enough to finish "A Little Help From My Friends." The song's last word jumped an entire octave. Reportedly McCartney stood next to Starr willing him to reach for its final note. In the end, he did get high with a little help from his friends.

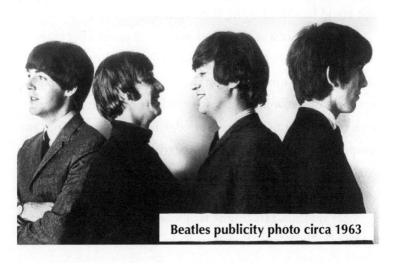

Beatles publicity photo circa 1963

INFLUENCES: MUSIC HALL, MOTOWN & DYLAN

Lennon and McCartney were crazy about '50s rock. Elvis ignited a fire in Lennon, and Buddy Holly was McCartney's muse. The Beatles moniker is a tribute to Holly's group, The Crickets. They pored over imported American records, learning every track of Little Richard and Chuck Berry albums. The Beatles' rock 'n' roll repertoire included 1933 swing instrumental "Moonglow" and Fats Domino's 1955 R&B shaker "Ain't That A Shame."

For the first five years (1957–1962) the Beatles were essentially a cover band. Their early core repertoire included American rocker Gene Vincent's "Blue-Jean Bop" and Roy Orbison's "Blue Angel." One of McCartney's most requested covers was "Till There Was You" which came from the 1957 Broadway musical *The Music Man*. He sang the 1960 ballad "A Taste Of Honey" seven times on BBC radio programs and reprised the song on the Beatles' first album. The Beatles played material as diverse as "Ain't She Sweet" and "Over The Rainbow." McCartney said he learned "Rainbow" from a Gene Vincent album, never knowing it was Judy Garland's signature song.

One of George Harrison's indirect influences was virtuoso guitarist Mickey Baker, who played on both soul singer Ray Charles' and The Coasters' records. Baker's innovative guitar solos influenced Buddy Holly's style and Harrison learned

Buddy's classic lead riffs. The Beatles covered Holly's "Words of Love" on their 1964 *Beatles For Sale* album.

A 1960 set list written by Paul McCartney for a concert at the Grosvenor Ballroom is the earliest document showing the Beatles performing one of their own songs, "One After 909." The Grosvenor Ballroom is located in Wallasey, Northen England just across the River Mersey from Liverpool. There were 25 songs on Grosvenor set list including "That's Allright Mama," "Tutti Fruti," "Kansas City," "Honey Don't," "Clarabella," "Stuck On You." "Sure To Fall," "Cathy's Clown," and "Long Tall Sally."

Fifteen Beatles Cover Songs

The Beatles' early repertoire was mostly written by other songwriters including cover songs "Money (That's What I Want)," "Baby It's You" and "Devil In Her Heart" which were featured on three of their first four LPs' and they played non-originals on all their international tours. Here's a hybrid mix of influential Beatles covers:

1. The Beatles performed a dozen or more Elvis songs including 1952's "Hound Dog" and 1957's "Let's Have a Party." Lennon said Elvis was his musical inspiration. The band met and jammed with Elvis in 1965 at his Beverly Hills home.
2. Little Richard's version of "Kansas City" (written by Wilbert Harrison) is on the *Beatles For Sale* album. They also played "Long Tall Sally" and "Slippin' and Slidin'."

3. "Hippy Hippy Shake" by Chad Romero was one of Lennon's big numbers. It's included on the band's *Live At The BBC* album.

4. "I Remember You" is available on *Live! at the Star-Club; Hamburg, Germany 1962*.

5. Phil Spector's 1958 song "To Know Him Is To Love Him" was part of the band 's Cavern, Hamburg and Decca set lists. The Beatles changed "him to her" in the song's lyrics.

6. "You've Got To Make A Fool Out Of Somebody" by Sonny James was R&B's first waltz and a template for future Beatles originals.

7. The Beatles perform Arthur Alexander's 1961 "A Shot Full of Rhythm & Blues on their *Live at the BBC* album.

8. In Hamburg, McCartney was known for stretching out Ray Charles' 1959 song " What I'd Say" for chorus after chorus.

9. "Twist and Shout" was originally called "Shake It Up Baby" when The Top Notes recorded it in 1961.

10. Paul McCartney sang lead on "Red Red Robin," made famous by Bing Crosby in 1926.

11. "Carolina Moon" was a country waltz originally sung by Connie Francis. It reached No.1 on the British charts.

12. Lennon often reprised Nat King Coles' 1958 song "Don't Blame Me."

13. McCartney sang the 1937 ballad "My Funny Valentine." The song was originally written for Broadway musical *Babes In Arms*.

14. The band admired songwriter Carl Perkins. They included his songs "Everybody's Trying To Be My Baby" and "Honey Don't" on the Beatles' fourth Parlophone album.
15. "Mr. Moonlight" was first recorded in 1962 by bluesman Piano Red. It appeared on the *Beatles For Sale* album.

Music Hall

British Music Hall songs were rapid fire, working class sing-alongs. The Victorian era musical style rose from London's 'hard scrabble' East End and featured upbeat, multiple verse melodies that often had bawdy lyrics or laughed at the British upper class. Music Hall acts were featured throughout England in 1940s-50s, including Liverpool's Hippodrome Theater, where Paul McCartney's father worked as a spotlight operator. Jim McCartney exposed his sons to his collection of 78 rpm Music Hall records and Paul (in his mid-teens) composed Beatles song "When I'm Sixty-Four" with a similar cabaret flair. Lennon & McCartney's early Beatles song "I Saw Her Standing There" is highlighted by its cheeky lyrical twist. McCartney sings, "She was just seventeen," and then Lennon's lyric winks, "If you know what I mean."

In the song "Sgt. Pepper's Lonely Hearts Club Band," the Beatles re-imagined themselves as cast members in a psychedelic variety show. John Lennon's song, "For the Benefit of Mr. Kite" adds waltz time to its swirling circus rhythm. Both tunes could have tumbled from a Music Hall stage. Many of Lennon & McCartney's compositions had sing along style choruses including "With A Little Help From My Friends," "All You Need Is Love" "Your Mother Should Know," "Lovely Rita," "Honey Pie," "Maxwell's Silver Hammer," "Yellow Submarine" and "All Together Now."

The Beatles weren't the only British Invasion band to incorporate the variety style into their songs. The Kink's "Dedicated Follower of Fashion," "Sunny Afternoon" and "Dandy" have Music Hall elements. Herman's Hermit's lead singer Peter Noone reprised "I'm Henry the Eight I Am" (pronounced 'Eery' with a cockney accent) which had been written in 1910 and sung by crooner Harry Champion. The Hermit's 1965 rendition became their second No.1 Hit on the US Billboard Hot 100 chart.

Paul McCartney's clever ten-line couplet pokes fun at the Queen of England. "Her Majesty" is a cabaret parody that slyly mocks the royal class. The sprightly snippet trails Abbey Road's opus "The End," the final song on the last sequential album recorded by the Beatles.

Motown Sounds

In a 2012 Public Broadcasting Service television documentary, McCartney stated that early Beatles originals reflected Motown's sound. He said America hadn't fully experienced Detroit's music, which allowed the Beatles to reshuffle its soulful vibration. Motown artists toured England regularly, often playing shows in Liverpool. The Beatles shared the stage with soul superstar Mary

Wells in 1964 and covered The Marvettes' 1961 song "Please Mr. Postman" on their first album.

McCartney said they borrowed gospel-influenced "call-and-response" techniques used by Detroit groups including The Shirelles. Beatles song "You're Going To Lose That Girl" features Lennon calling out a warning with McCartney and Harrison responding/repeating Lennon's advice. As a solo artist, McCartney would record with Motown artists Stevie Wonder and Michael Jackson.

Dylan

Bob Dylan's influence on the Beatles' songwriting had several unusual twists. He first met the band on their 1964 American tour and decided to "turn on" with them. He mistakenly thought "I Want To Hold Your Hand" included the lyrics, "I get high..." when the Beatles were actually singing about trying to hide. It was the first time the Beatles tried marijuana and it soon became the psychedelic frosting on their musical palate.

It's unlikely the Beatles knew Dylan's real name was Robert Allan Zimmerman or that he borrowed his talking blues style from Woody Guthrie, the 1930s dust bowl singer. Guthrie, in turn, had likely heard 'spoken' vocals on the 1926 recordings of Southern entertainer Chris Bouchillion. The Beatles listened to Dylan's dialogue-driven stories and rambling song-poems repeatedly during their 1964 musical residency in Paris. His dark metaphors inspired Lennon to write about his own shadows.

Dylan's influence is heard on Lennon songs "Nowhere Man," "In My Life" and "Norwegian Wood." All three appeared on the band's 1965 *Rubber Soul* album. In 1966 Dylan released an opaque, parody of "Norwegian Wood" titled "Fourth Time Around." It was included on his *Blonde On Blonde* LP. In subsequent interviews, Lennon said he wasn't amused by Dylan's jarring caricature.

Inspiration

The pace of the Beatles' recording schedule was astounding. From 1963 to 1966 (*Please Please Me* through *Revolver*), they released seven LP albums and six double sided single records. This output was in addition to playing hundreds of concerts including international tours, live radio/television appearances and filming both *A Hard Day's Night* and *Help* feature films.

Once dubbed "The Laziest Man In England" by the British press, John Lennon also found time to write and illustrate two books of experimental fiction. *In His Own Write* was published in 1964 and *A Spaniard in the Works* in 1965.

In the beginning, the Beatles' lyrical messages were simple and straightforward. Their songs described the shape and circumstances of love. What made early originals "She Loves You" and "All My Loving" striking were their pleasing harmonies and compelling arrangements. As their success grew, the pressure to create new music became intense, and songwriting became an occupation. Lennon and McCartney often sat side-by-side at McCartney's London home trying out chord combinations and lyrical ideas.

Ringo Starr commented in the *Beatles Anthology* that they never scheduled rehearsal time to practice new material because their songs were finished in the recording studio. He said the band's songwriters would first play simple acoustic versions of their creations for producer Martin. Then they would work out complex instrumental passages, fine-tune lyrics and add their signature blended harmonies.

Beatles Stories:
60's rock singer JAY FERGUSON

Foo Fighters lead guitarist/singer Dave Grohl, bassist Chris Hillman of *The Birds* and Jay Ferguson, lead vocalist of 60's bands *Spirit and Jo Jo Gunne* each said the Beatles inspired them to become musicians. In 1967 Jay Ferguson's band Spirit charted a No.1 USA Hit with "I Got A Line One You" and his 1978 solo hit "Thunder Island" with Joe Walsh on electric guitar, reached No.9 on the Billboard Chart. In 2007, Ferguson wrote the award winning theme to NBC Television's "The Office" and in 2014 he spoke with me in Summerland, CA about how the Beatles influenced his songwriting."

Q: What was your first memory of the Beatles?

Jay Ferguson: I remember going to the 1964 movie *A Hard Day's Night*. Everybody has their own story about seeing that film. Mine was kind of funny because we saw it a drive-in, not a theater packed with girls. My friend and I were watching it and saying, 'This is awesome.' Then I remember rolling down the window and from about two hundred cars you heard this muffled screaming inside… what a weird sound! The Beatles made it possible to accept pop music. That was revolutionary. Here's this new sound, here's a new look, a new haircut, a new culture. They just opened this path, so it was a huge impact.

Q: How did they shape their early songs?

Ferguson: When I first listened to the Beatles they were still doing traditional song form: introduction, verse, chorus, bridge. Between the Beatles, the Kinks and some of the Who, that's where I learned my first songwriting chops. The ABCs of how you put a song together and how you work in that three minutes or less format. How you tell your story and how you create your art — it was all guitar-driven. I loved that.

Q: And then the Beatles began to stretch their musical canvas.

Ferguson: The Beatles were just always a step ahead. Then they started messing with song form, putting 3/4 time in the middle of a song or doing something really linear, like George Harrison songs that just stayed in one spot. They started breaking the rules and lyrically too. It was like — OK! That changed the structure of songs, what they were saying and how they were written. That really was happening in Spirit. It showed up in our first 1968 record big time.

Q: You had more freedom to express yourselves...

Ferguson: It was almost a dare. There wouldn't have been Spirit's *The Twelve Dreams of Dr. Sardonicus* without it. It's probably the record we were most proud of. It was a concept album and carried the Spirit imprint of 'we're doing this, we're going psychedelic and we're into space and jazz.' It was kind of like we'd found out how to do that. It was the peak of our craft.

Q: What sparks your songwriting?

Ferguson: It's like writing novels. Part of it is getting up every day and sitting at the typewriter. It's picking up the guitar or picking at the piano and really trying to open up to the muse. That spark, it's a melody or something unique that just starts the motor running. You don't make songs — they just get dropped down on you. I'm convinced if you're open enough you go, 'Oh, here it comes.' Songs, like writing a novel, have characters that start writing themselves. They start to come alive.

Q: Have you deconstructed the Beatles songs?

Ferguson: The Beatles had a cone of suspended reality around them. It went on for years after they disbanded. For me there's been a *Wizard of Oz* moment with the Beatles music where the curtain is pulled back. I create music, so I know how it's recorded and written. So now, rather than be struck by the wonder of it all, I go in and say 'I see what they're doing here. I see the mechanics of this.' The Beatles have come down from Olympus to being brilliant musicians.

Q: Has their legacy shifted over the decades?

Ferguson: The Beatles' legacy will never change, because of their songs. I saw the Eagles documentary, and it's always about a band's music. The Beatles will never come off the top of that list. If you go from the first to last record, you can find everything in their music. It's like Bach. You can find Schoenberg in Bach. You can find Brahms in it. The Beatles baked everything into their cake.

INNOVATIONS: EXPERIMENTS & ELEVATION

Sir George Martin

No two Beatles songs sounded alike. Producer George Martin helped crystallize the Beatles guitar-driven sound by adding sophisticated orchestral arrangements and classical instrumentation. Under his guidance the Beatles-fueled art rock's renaissance, stretching boundaries and expanding pop's soundscape. In 1996, the Queen of England recognized Martin's musical contributions by granting him Knighthood. Before joining EMI in 1950, Sir George studied piano and oboe at London's Guildhall School of Music and Drama. His oboe instructor was Margaret Eliot, mother of actress Jane Asher. After interviewing the Beatles at Royal Albert Hall in 1963, Asher became McCartney's long-term girlfriend and then fiancé.

Martin produced dozens of classical and comedy albums before auditioning the Liverpool quartet. He was fourteen years older than Lennon, but they quickly developed musical rapport. Lennon followed his advice to speed-up the tempo of "Please Please Me," and it became their first No. 1 UK Hit. McCartney held the top note for twelve beats, and Lennon delivered the song's driving melody line.

Lennon and McCartney sometimes brought Martin nearly complete songs, including "I Want To Hold Your Hand," but Sir George soon became their musical interpreter. He penned the arrangement for the string quartet used in McCartney's song "Yesterday" and the octet score for "Eleanor Rigby," which appeared on the band's Revolver album. He also performed on selected Beatles tracks, including the baroque inspired half-speed piano solo on Lennon's "In My Life," adding keyboards on McCartney's bouncing "Lovely Rita" and playing harpsichord on *Sgt. Pepper* track "Fixing A Hole."

With the exception of the band's 1970 album *Let It Be*, George Martin's bond with the Beatles was virtually unbreakable. From 1962–69, he was their primary record producer and remained with the band from single "Love Me Do" through *Abbey Road* song "The End." It was a remarkable run of hits.

Beginnings & Endings

The Beatles most remembered opening chord may be Harrison's F with a G on top. The resonant introduction begins "A Hard Day's Night." A closer hearing shows that Harrison had some help. His echoing twelve-string vibration also contains a McCartney plucked bass note and Lennon's single picked electric string.

The Beatles held the top five spots on the Billboard Chart in April 1964.

Many of the band's early songs begin without instruments. "If I Fell" tumbles out in an unexpected interval with Lennon singing the chorus. On "I'm a Loser," Lennon's moan is quickly joined by McCartney's tenor. The song closes with a fade-out instrumental jam.

The Beatles' variations seemed endless. They used feedback on the opening strains of "I Feel Fine," and early original "Ask Me Why" has a smooth bossa nova groove. Lennon's solo vocal jump-starts "No Reply," and the song ends on Harrison's minor guitar chord. "Do What You're Doing" begins with Ringo's drum solo. The bridge in Lennon and McCartney's 1964 song "Baby's In Black" contains a harmonic jump never heard before or since in pop music. Lennon later experimented with drone chords and recorded guitar progressions backwards.

Long & Short

The shortest Beatles song is McCartney's twenty-three second serenade "Her Majesty," found on the band's *Abbey Road* LP. The group's longest song is on the *White Album*; the eight-minute, twenty-two second opus, "Revolution #9." Lennon and Yoko Ono's sound collage was designed to be an experimental canvas painted with variant audio effects.

Single releases including "I Want To Hold Your Hand," "Paperback Writer," "Rain" and "Lady Madonna" never appeared on the band's original Parlophone LPs. EMI's American label assembled albums with out-of-sequence singles and previously issued Parlophone tracks. Capitol Records' compendium releases ended with the world wide roll-out of 1967's *Sgt. Pepper's Lonely Hearts Club Band*.

Varispeed Recording

EMI's audio engineers experimented with Varispeed techniques, which increases or slows the tape speed during the recording process. John Lennon's "Strawberry Fields Forever" combined two separate versions of the song recorded in different keys and at varying speeds. The song was edited at its one minute mark and combined Take 7 with Take 26. This tape edit was accomplished by lowering the speed of Take 26 by 11.5 percent. The use of Varispeed brought the song's final mix into almost exactly the same key.

Another example of the use of Varispeed occurred during George Martin's piano solo on song "In My Life." It was recorded at half-speed and then played back at the normal tape cycle, which produced a harpsichord sounding effect. The vocals and backing tracks to songs "Lucy In The Sky With Diamonds" and "Magical Mystery Tour were also created by using Varispeed tape manipulation.

It's remarkable that EMI's engineers were able to imagine such innovative recording solutions given 1960's rudimentary technology, compared with today's multi-track recording devices. The *Sgt. Pepper's Lonely Hearts Club Band* album took three months and seven hundred hours of studio time to record on a Studer J37 four-track deck. Ten of the fourteen tracks on the Beatles first album "Please Please Me" were recorded in one 13-hour marathon session on a two-track BTR tape machine.

Artificial Double Tracking (ADT)

Lennon asked EMI engineer Ken Townsend if he could thicken his voice without recording a duplicate vocal track. Beginning with the *Revolver* album, Townsend created an exact copy of Lennon's voice by delaying the tape machine's magnetic signal. He shaped a combined vocal track by mixing the new track with Lennon's original vocal recording. He called the process Artificial Double Tracking. ADT technology was used on Beatles songs including "Fixing A Hole," "I Am The Walrus" and Harrison's "While My Guitar Gently Weeps."

Riffs

Many of the Beatles songs had compelling guitar solos, but only a handful were truly riff driven. Riffs are rock fills that envelop and define a song. "Day Tripper" and "Paperback Writer" both feature dominant guitar solos doubled by McCartney's bass lines. They're signature Beatles riffs. The *White Album*'s "Birthday" is dominated by its repeating hard rock attack. McCartney plays the song's shredding guitar solo. His boogie-woogie piano riff frames "Lady Madonna." Other notable Beatles riffs include George Harrison's guitar work on "Here Comes The Sun."

Direct Box or Not?

The invention of the Direct Box (sometimes called direct injection) provided a linear route to the recording console. It eliminated the need to constantly mic bass or guitar amplifiers. McCartney plugged his bass directly into a small electronic box, which boosted its signal before sending it to the tape deck. Direct Box recording allowed him to play rhythm guitar live on *Sgt. Pepper*'s title backing track. He later replaced Lennon's temporary bass line with one of his own.

In his memoir *Here, There and Everywhere*, EMI engineer Geoff Emerick said he rarely used the Direct Box. *Sgt. Pepper*'s engineer stated the reason McCartney's bass lines sounded fuller was because of microphone experimentation. Emerick said he re-wired a speaker cabinet making it into a large microphone and then placed the re-converted mic directly against the bass amplifier, creating the thumping Detroit Motown-style pulse McCartney sought.

Cross Fades & Tape Loops

Several of the tracks on *Sgt. Pepper* are separated by less than a second. The LP's opening song ends with a key change that cross fades directly into "A Little Help From My Friends." One song seamlessly becomes another. A similar fade-in technique is used to begin "A Day In The Life." It slowly evolves from a single-strummed acoustic guitar chord.

Song transitions took a wild turn on the band's 1968 *White Album*. Track-to-track connections included a slamming door, scattered applause and laughter, various tape loops, flamenco guitar musings and Lennon-esque mutterings. The album's songs were also linked by McCartney's un-copyrighted repeating vocal, "Can you take me back?" and Ringo Starr screaming his fingers were on fire.

The Beatles created sounds rock fans had never heard before. It seemed their musical alchemy was never-ending. After the band stopped touring in 1966, members spent months perfecting their new studio recordings. Listening to a Beatles album became an astonishing and intoxicating experience. Their creations used the mellotron, Moog synthesizer, fuzz-boxes, wah-wah pedals and exotic instruments from India, including the harmonium, swarmadel and sitar.

**Wings guitarist Laurence Juber at the
2014 Fest for Beatles Fans**

Ravi Shankar's final concert in
Long Beach, CA, 11-4-12

THE SITAR'S SOUND

Rock fans likely first heard Indian music on the Beatles' *Rubber Soul* album. In late October 1965, George Harrison threaded a sitar melody into John Lennon's song "Norwegian Wood (This Bird Has Fown)." Harrison was introduced to the sitar by members of The Byrds who recorded at the same Los Angeles studio used by India's most accomplished sitarist Ravi Shankar.

Harrison's use of the sitar was preceded by Indian-influenced songs including The Yardbird's June 1965 "Heart Full of Soul" and The Kink's July 1965 song "See My Friends." Kink's guitarist Ray Davies used 12-string guitar feedback to simulate Indian drone chords and added a sitar-like lead at the beginning and end of the song. Davies began writing "See My Friends" during the band's tour stop over in Bombay, India.

Ragas

The sitar evolved from a Persian instrument called the setar, which meant "three strings." A modern sitar has up to twenty-two strings but only seven are used for playing melody. The remaining fifteen provide accompaniment and sound similar to an exotic auto harp when played together. Indian compositions are called *ragas*. There are no key changes like those found in western music. Ragas provide a melodic framework which allows the sitarist to improvise and interact, while supporting instruments add color and pulse.

Harrison studied with Shankar in London and India but soon learned the sitar would take years to master, but the duo's mentor/rock star collaboration was mutually beneficial. Harrison's new musical vision expanded the Beatles creative template and Shankar became a successful touring artist. He played at the Monterey Pop Festival in 1967, Woodstock in 1969 and the Concert for Bangladesh in 1971, held at Madison Square Garden in New York City.

The *Sgt. Pepper* album included Harrison's pivotal composition "Within You, Without You," which was based on a Shankar raga that Harrison modified and shortened. The song was recorded in three separate sections and spliced together. Other Indian-influenced Beatles' songs include *Revolver*'s "Tomorrow Never Knows," which flowed from a single drone chord, and "Love To You," featuring the tambura, percussive tabia and sitar. Harrison also played an Indian sarod on his single release, "The Inner Light," and tambura on Lennon's gem, "Across The Universe." Lennon's lyrical masterpiece first appeared on a charity album benefiting the World Wildlife Fund.

I was fortunate to hear and photograph Ravi Shankar's final concert at the Terrace Theater in Long Beach, CA. Shankar played by instinct, rhythmically plucking and bending the ornate instrument 's metal strings. He was accompanied by two drone-stringed tamburas, a wooden flute and percussionists playing tabla and dholka drum. His thirty-five-year-old daughter Anoushka joined him on second sitar. She had studied with her father since eight years of age and is now an international touring artist. Shankar's other daughter is jazz-pop recording artist Nora Jones.

The Rolling Stones and Donovan used sitar to shape their '60s hits. Stones guitarist Brian Jones plucked it on "Paint It Black," and Donovan used the expressive instrument on "Sunshine Superman." Musicians as diverse as Elton John, Metallica, Beck, REM and Shakira have recorded songs with Indian textures. Since then the sitar has slowly returned to its classical raga roots. Perhaps contemporary rock will re-imagine its stirring sound. Ravi Shankar will be smiling.

RISHIKESH

August 24, 1967

His name was Maharishi Mahesh Yogi. Dressed in white silk, he sat cross-legged on a dais decorated with bright flowers. The yogi's long hair flowed over his shoulders and his full beard was peppered with grey. Maharishi's serene smile and high-pitched laughter charmed his listeners. In the audience that night were John Lennon, Paul McCartney, George

Harrison and their wives and friends. Ringo Starr had stayed home to help with his newborn son.

After receiving a physics degree from India's Allahabad University in 1942, Maharishi became a disciple of spiritual master Swami Brahmananda. Shortly before his death in 1953, the famed swami named Maharishi as his successor. At his London lecture, the yogi joyfully explained that one could travel beyond conscious thought by repeating a selected mantra. He called the technique Transcendental Meditation®.

After the Hilton lecture, Lennon, McCartney and Harrison met Maharishi backstage and agreed to accompany him by train to his seminar in Bangor, Wales. Starr also decided to come along. Upon arrival, the Beatles discovered they didn't have enough money on hand to pay for their dinner at an Indian restaurant. The café's owner had never heard of the band and demanded immediate payment. Luckily Harrison was able to pry a twenty pound note from the sole of his sandals that he kept for emergencies. The next day the band received word that their long-time personal manager Brian Epstein had died of an accidental prescription drug overdose. Epstein had taken care of everything for the group, from investing their earnings to arranging tropical vacations. He was their trusted banker, booker and fixer.

In *The Beatles Anthology*, McCartney remarked that they felt empty after Epstein's death. The band was suddenly adrift and in need of a new touchstone. The Beatles had traversed the drug scene and were primed for an inward journey. They readily accepted Maharishi's invitation to attend his twelve-week deep meditation course in Rishikesh, India.

The Ashram

Maharishi's retreat was a six-hour drive from New Delhi that took travelers back hundreds of years. The road to Rishikesh was shared by horse-drawn carts, holy men dressed in loincloths, sacred wandering cows and the aroma of incense and spices. The fourteen acre ashram was set on a hillside in "The Valley of the Saints," home to dozens of spiritual schools. Its location offered striking views of the Ganges River and the small town of Rishikesh. The retreat was surrounded by a lush teak forest concealing bright parakeets, shrill peacocks, monkeys, pythons and wild elephants. Guests were advised to stay inside the ashram's fenced boundaries.

John Lennon, George Harrison and their wives arrived on February 16, 1968. Paul McCartney and girlfriend Jane Asher came several days later. Ringo Starr and wife Maureen decided to travel at the last minute but only stayed two weeks. They pined for their young children and discovered the retreat wasn't like a British holiday camp. The remaining Beatles were joined by fellow meditators Donovan, Beach Boys singer Mike Love and jazz flutist Paul Horn.

Revelations

To their fans, the Beatles' journey to India was mythic and magical. The faraway continent was beyond imagination's reach. It seemed unfathomable that the world's most famous band had dropped out to meditate. Fans were mystified and wondered if Transcendental Meditation® was the genesis of a new religion and how it might change the group's music.

Over fifty meditation students were on site when the Beatles arrived. They included a croupier from Las Vegas, a faith healer from Germany, an American actor and followers from Sweden and Lebanon. All hoped to become meditation instructors. Also present was American Nancy Cooke De Herrera, who was Maharishi's liaison with those attending the Rishikesh course. She had been initiated into meditation six years earlier and was present for many of Lennon's and Harrison's Rishikesh conversations with Maharishi. She wrote about their sudden departure from the ashram in her 1993 book, *Beyond Gurus*.

Farrow Sisters

Courting celebrities became Maharishi's blind spot. Neither the Beatles, nor other well-known musical artists or acclaimed actors, were ever charged a fee to attend the yogi's courses. Maharishi defended his decision by saying famous musicians and actors brought positive publicity and helped draw others to the movement. The Beatles and their wives had posed with the yogi in a 1967 issue of *Life Magazine*.

Prior to the Beatles' arrival, actress Mia Farrow and her sister Prudence had left the ashram under a cloud. Maharishi had paid for both sisters' travel expenses and reportedly was star-struck in their presence. Farrow confided to Cooke de Herrera she believed the yogi had made a pass at her. She said he started to stroke her hair during a punja ceremony at his private residence. Cooke de Herrera assured Farrow that touching a student's hair was a part of the ritual, an honor Maharishi had bestowed upon her. Farrow wouldn't hear any further explanation and immediately left the ashram, only to return shortly after the Beatles arrived.

Mantras & Songs

The retreat was constructed around six tiers of rooms, grouped together with a large lecture hall and dining room. Maharishi brought in special items to furnish the Beatles' accommodations, including poster beds and thick carpeting. Their showers had hot water but the hand-carved toilet seats covered a hole in the ground. It wasn't a Hilton hotel suite, but the band's lodgings were upgraded compared to those of other meditation students.

The yogi's personal residence and ashram was constructed with a $100,000 gift from tobacco heiress Doris Duke. After her donation was leaked to the press, Ms. Duke left the meditation movement and never returned. Maharishi's stylish home had tiled floors and a rooftop deck used for entertaining and providing instruction to invited guests.

The Beatles settled into the ashram's daily rhythm, attending lectures and eating their meals with other students. The band's arrival had been closely monitored by the international press, but Maharishi promised the Beatles they would not be disturbed during their stay. True to his word, he had the ashram's fence line patrolled by a former Indian Gurkha soldier. Harrison's wife, Pattie Boyd, described their eight weeks at the ashram as "serene and peaceful."

Between meditation sessions, the Beatles had time to compose music on the acoustic guitars they brought along. Harrison continued his sitar studies with a local Indian teacher and Donovan wrote one of his most memorable melodies, "Jennifer Juniper," at the ashram. Mike Love helped germinate Beach Boy-style harmonies for McCartney's song "Back In the U.S.S.R.," and Donovan taught Lennon and McCartney new finger-picking styles. Although few of the Beatles *White Album* songs have Indian textures, many of the 1968 album's tracks were either written or begun at the ashram.

Alternate Endings

McCartney and his girlfriend, actress Jane Asher, left Rishikesh after six weeks because of her theatrical commitments. Donovan then departed to begin a concert tour, and Mia Farrow flew to England to make a film with actor Richard Burton. She reportedly left in high spirits and spoke of joining the yogi in Kashmir. The two remaining Beatles discussed helping expand the movement's international reach.

Lennon envisioned building a television station at the ashram to broadcast the yogi's wisdom around the globe. Maharishi wanted to construct an airport near the retreat. Harrison was enthusiastic about staging a major musical event in New Delhi, India featuring the Beatles, Donovan and Ravi Shankar.

Both Lennon and Harrison wanted to immediately begin filming a documentary about the yogi's teachings. Lennon asked Maharishi's liaison to phone Apple Corps' Managing Director Neil Aspinall and have him gather the needed movie-making equipment. Maharishi was pleased with the plan until Cooke de Herrera reminded him that he had already committed to a documentary with another film company. The yogi said there would be enough work for all, but told her to send Aspinall a cable requesting Apple Corps delay filming.

Intervention

On April 12, 1968, Lennon and Harrison (with their wives and entourage) left Rishikesh in a storm. Lennon had confronted the yogi about his alleged sexual encounter with an unnamed American girl. He would later sing about Maharishi's human failings in *White Album* song "Sexy Sadie." Cooke de Herrera believes there may have been another reason for their exodus.

Shortly before Lennon's explosion, Four Star Film's attorney had visited the retreat and left with a signed contract to produce the yogi's documentary. When the competing movie crew arrived to begin filming, Lennon and Harrison left in a fury — the same day. Was it coincidence or consequence? Lennon was later quoted in the *Los Angeles Times*, stating he was disappointed by the guru's focus on financial gain.

Epilogue

No proof ever surfaced of Maharishi's alleged sexual indiscretion. Some of those present in Rishikesh have speculated that Beatles' entourage member Alex Madras fabricated the story or a jealous meditation student had made up the fantasy. George Harrison personally apologized to the yogi and John Lennon later said he continued to practice meditation. Ringo Starr and Paul McCartney still raise funds for Transcendental Meditation® research and education.

Without the Beatles' participation, the Four Star Film footage shot at the ashram and in Kashmir was never released as a documentary. It was reportedly left in a Los Angeles film vault and eventually deteriorated due to the effects of time and neglect. If you return to Rishikesh today, you can glimpse the remains of the fabled retreat. Most of the original buildings have been reclaimed by dense forest, but the hillside meditation caves are still visible. Perhaps visitors can imagine a time when the Beatles' music and Maharishi's deep meditation fit together in nearly perfect harmony.

MOMENTS

When I was granted an interview with the son of the world's most famous rock singer, I drafted an opening question and let the short interview flow. Setting my nerves aside, I found Paul McCartney's son James to be calm and less guarded than I anticipated, almost smiling during our short photo session.

I unknowingly conducted the last interview with Apple Records recording artist Jackie Lomax. He passed away several months after our meeting in Ojai, CA. From Yoko Ono's novel contributions to the Rock Hall to 60's British songwriter Mitch Murray, each of the following interviews illuminates a Beatles moment.

James McCartney 2013

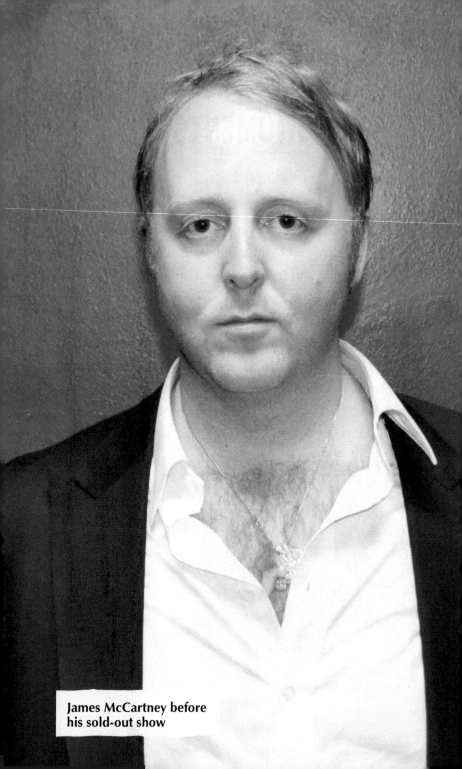

James McCartney before
his sold-out show

BACKSTAGE WITH JAMES MCCARTNEY

Legacy is defined as something left behind. Musicians often give their sons and daughters gifts of passion and purpose. Paul McCartney and his wife Linda raised daughters Heather, Mary and Stella. Their careers have included photography, ceramics and design. Stella owns seventeen fashion boutiques spread across the world. McCartney and Heather Mills daughter Beatrice is now fifteen. Ringo Starr's only daughter Lee is also a fashion designer.

Each of the Beatles' five sons has become a working musician and/or recording artist. Julian Lennon released his debut pop album *"Valotte"* in 1984. John Lennon's second son, Sean, formed the band Ghost of a Saber Tooth Tiger in 2008. He recently joined Primus bassist Les Claypool to record as The Claypool Lennon Delirium. The duo's 2016 tour included a powerful cover of the Beatles' psychedelic-flavored "Tomorrow Never Knows," composed by Sean's father.

George Harrison's son Dhani fronts rock act thenewno2 and has collaborated with songwriter Ben Harper in pop-up band Fist Full of Mercy. Ringo's first son, Zak Starkey, is The Who's permanent tour drummer and has performed at the Super Bowl and London's Olympics. Ringo's second son, Jason Starkey, is also a drummer who has played with UK rock groups including Musty Jack Sponge and the Exploding Nudists.

In 2013 James McCartney (Paul's only son) toured America, playing forty-seven concerts in twenty-seven states. At his Santa Barbara, CA, show, McCartney accompanied himself on the grand piano (decorated with lighted faux candles) and played originals on several alternately tuned acoustic guitars. The generous set-list included material from his debut album and a revealing cover of Neil Young's song "Old Man." McCartney's fluid finger picking and emotive vocals propelled his performance. The thirty-nine-year-old songwriter shares his father's oval facial features and piercing eyes. I interviewed and photographed McCartney backstage before his sold-out show.

Q: How did you develop the upper reaches of your voice?

James McCartney: Good coaching, I think. Dad taught me a lot growing up. Beatles songs like "Helter Skelter" and "Oh Darling" have that high raw octave. They're real screamers. I also went through a Nirvana phase. That was a big influence. I read that Curt Cobain would go fishing with his friends and then go off on his own to scream. Those kinds of things inspire me.

Q: Your song "Angel" has a great groove. How did it evolve?

McCartney: I was going to write a song like Cobain's "Smells Like Teen Spirit" but it turned out completely different. I wanted to write something that felt good.

The idea of meeting your true love and being content and happy. It's all about love at first sight.

Then McCartney turned the table on me. I asked him to detail the instrumentation on his new studio album but he responded, "What did you hear?" Luckily I'd listened to the tracks and crafted an on-the-spot response about the song's varied textures. McCartney just sipped his backstage cocktail and listened to me. After I'd finished he nodded and said, "Yeah, that's about what I was shooting for." Then I asked him a follow-up question.

Q: How did your new album Me come together?

McCartney: It's acoustically influenced with a bit of electronica. I listen to blues a lot, rootsy kind of stuff. The new album is trying to be rock 'n' roll, mainly. That's what I'm going toward. On this solo tour, I sometimes feel like Bob Dylan in a good way. I'm out there on my own, but I'm not trumpeting myself — that's an English phrase. (laughter)

Q: Last question: How do you view the Beatles' musical legacy?

McCartney: It's limitless, infinite, and spiritual. It's timeless (he motioned with his hand). It's everything, isn't it? The Beatles were classic, pure rock. They raised the bar.

(*Note*: James McCartney subsequently released his second studio album *The Blackberry Train* in 2016 and toured across Europe and the US.)

Mitch Murray 1962

ENGLISH SONGWRITER MITCH MURRAY

When Mitch Murray was twenty-two years old, his dad staked him for a year to make it in the music business. With remarkable timing, Murray had his first No.1 UK Hit one year later. Murray wrote or co-wrote four chart-topping pop hits in the 1960s/70s for British bands Gerry and the Pacemakers, Freddie and the Dreamers and Paper Lace. He received two *Ivor Novar Awards* presented by the British Academy of Songwriters, Composers and Authors. Rock musician Sting (Gordon Sumner) said Murray's bestselling 1964 book "*How To Write A Hit Song*" inspired him to become a songwriter.

I spoke by phone with Murray in 2016 at his home on the Isle of Man. "In the 1960s we needed singers and they needed us. I played ukulele and when you just have four or five chords to work with, you're forced to come up with strong melodies," he said. Murray then recounted how one of his songs nearly became the Beatles first single record.

Q: How did your song "How Do You Do It?" make its way to the Beatles?

Mitch Murray: I made my demo recordings cheaply at a studio called Regent Sound in London. The Rolling

Stones recorded their first album there. After the place closed at night, the sound engineers would make extra money doing demos. It cost about thirty pounds ($84 US) to record two or three new songs in 1962. "How Do You Do It?" was one of those early demos.

English songwriter Barry Mason ended up singing lead on "How Do You Do It?" and he invited me to bring that demo and several other new songs up to EMI. I hadn't charted any records at that time but a few had made money as B sides. Music publisher Dick James listened to my songs and ironically said another tune, "Better Luck Next Time," could be a big hit. I told him I wasn't ready to sign with a music publisher.

The next thing I knew there was a new singing group from Liverpool (The Beatles) and EMI/Parlophone producer George Martin was going to record them. Of all the new songs I'd written I thought "How Do You Do It?" was the best, but I wasn't happy about a new group doing my tune. I wanted a big artist to record it. British singer Johnny Angel had taken the song "Better Luck Next Time."

Q: Producer George Martin wanted your "best" song.

Murray: George Martin was a really honest, honorable, great bloke. Dick James told me that Martin wanted the Beatles to record "How Do You Do It?" as their first single. I hadn't heard them but he said they did harmonies like church hymns. I wanted someone who had already broken into the business. Dick James invited me down to hear the acetate demo the Beatles had made of my song. I thought it was terrible, kind of like they were 'sending it up.'

Q: How had the Beatles changed the song?

Murray: Some ways it was more feasible, but they put in some '*la las*' and that wasn't how I wrote it. I looked at Dick James. He remarked, 'I know, I know.' And I said, 'Dick, I can't let that song out. It deserves a lot better than this.' He remarked, 'I really have to agree with you.' Dick James called producer Martin who said the Beatles would have another go at it. I heard their original "Love Me Do" which was slotted for the single's B side. I thought it was pretty catchy but had amateur lyrics. My song had a bit more extra magic. Some people saw it and some didn't. With the Beatles, I can understand why they turned the song down, and maybe they understood why I turned them down. The decision was quite independent for both of us. We never spoke directly to each other.

Q: What was the song's next chapter?

Murray: The Beatles admitted they didn't put their all into my song. As it happened, it worked out beautifully for all of us. "Love Me Do" went on to establish them to stardom. The Beatles manager still believed in my song. Brian Epstein invited me up to Liverpool to have a chat. He was trying to woo me to have another singer record "How Do You Do It?"

While I was there I overheard Epstein speaking on the phone. I'll never forget it. He was talking to a promoter saying, 'No, No, No, that wouldn't be fair to the fans.' I really didn't have to hear more than that. It was a wonderful reason to say no. It showed he was a man of integrity, a good guy. I was taken by that.

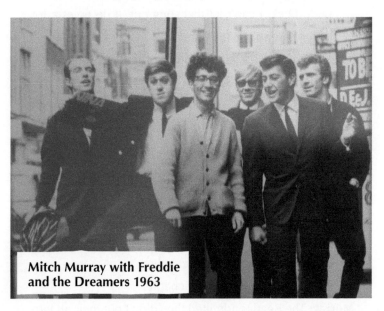

Mitch Murray with Freddie and the Dreamers 1963

Q: The singer Epstein had in mind was Liverpool vocalist Gerry Marsden.

Murray: Yes, Brian called him the 'British Bobby Darin.' I didn't want the Beatles to record "How Do You Do

It?" and they didn't want it anyway. We agreed to let Gerry have a shot. I still didn't have a publishing deal. Then I heard the Gerry and the Pacemakers' recording and said, 'Yes, that's wonderful. It's a great record! Where do I sign?'

Marsden's version of the song was more forceful. He was a very powerful singer and had a terrific presence. You put him in front of a microphone, and he would dominate it. George Martin backed him with a powerful arrangement. You could hear everything on the record. Marsden's nose was on the microphone. The song went to No.1 in the UK in April 1963 and was a Top Ten Hit in the USA in 1964.

Q: Did you talk with any of the Beatles after "How Do You Do It?" became a hit?

Murray: I saw Paul McCartney at Prince Charles' London home (Clarence House) at a get-together held by the Prince. We see each other every so often. Once on a flight to Berlin, Paul started singing "How Do You Do It?" from the front of the first class cabin. I'd also run into Ringo and George occasionally on television shows, but Paul most often. He was the melodist of the group. John was the more the beat and rhythmic side. He provided the atmosphere and power in their songs.

Q: You also wrote The Pacemakers' follow-up single.

Murray: I didn't know I was competing with John Lennon. One afternoon in Dick James' London office, Lennon jokingly threatened to 'F...ing thump me' if my next tune bested his. I'd written "I Like It" for Gerry and the Pacemakers and John was pitching his song "Hello Little Girl." The Pacemakers recorded both songs but only released "I Like It." In May, 1963, it became their second No.1 UK Hit but Lennon never laid a hand on me.[1]

Q: What happened after your first two hits for Gerry and the Pacemakers?

Murray: I had a call from an agent for British band Freddie and the Dreamers. He said lead singer Freddie Garrity had started the song "I'm Telling You Now" but needed help finishing it. He had written the first line and I helped him complete the melody. I also wrote the song's middle piece and ending. When they sent me the recording, the band's agent tried to get me to accept a seventy-five percent versus twenty-five percent split for publishing

---

1 "Hello Little Girl" was the first song John Lennon wrote in 1957. It became a UK Hit in August 1963 for Liverpool band The Foremost. The single was recorded during the Beatles' Decca Records audition in 1962 with Stuart Sutcliffe on bass but never released commercially by the Beatles until their 1995 *Anthology 1* CD. In 1964, Murray's song "I Like It" reached #17 on the American Billboard Chart.

royalties. I said, if Freddie's happy with twenty-five percent we have a deal! He slammed the phone down.

Q: That song had international success.

Murray: "I'm Telling You Now" went to No. 2 on the UK charts in 1963 and was a No. 1 Hit in the USA in 1965. In the end there were no hard feelings, although there were that day. Once in the early '60s I was riding the London Tube and heard someone whistling a song I'd written a few months earlier. Someone I didn't know. Yeah, that was a fabulous feeling.

ROCK HALL'S MEREDITH RUTLEDGE-BORGER

Rock & Roll Hall of Fame

In 1952, Cleveland, Ohio, DJ Alan Freed came up with three words that described the up-tempo, black R&B records he played. Freed's phrase changed everything. He called it "rock 'n' roll."

Forty years later that description helped inspire the city of Cleveland to build the Rock & Roll Hall of Fame. It opened in 1995 and is set on Lake Erie's south shore, near the revamped city center. Sunlight pours through its honeycomb design. The six-story Rock Hall houses the world's largest collection of rock memorabilia and artifacts.

The museum's exhibits examine rock's river of music, from early blues to Elvis and the British Invasion through modern pop/rock artists. Its artifacts include the Mellotron which McCartney played on the introduction to Lennon's song "Strawberry Fields Forever." Rock Hall Associate Curator Meredith Rutledge-Borger spoke with me about the museum's large Beatles collection.

Lennon's black Rickenbacker and Beatles performance suits at the Rock Hall

Lennon's illustrated Gibson acoustic guitar at the Rock Hall

Q: How did Yoko Ono help curate the Rock Hall's Beatles exhibit?

Meredith Rutledge-Borger: After her husband's murder in 1980, Yoko installed a white wall telephone next to the Beatles exhibition. It was a working phone and Yoko would occasionally call and talk with whoever picked it up. It's disconnected now, but it was remarkable of her to do that. As part of our permanent collection we have a number of John

Lennon's original lyrics and photographs taken during their peace protests and Bed-Ins. We also have the Gibson acoustic guitar Lennon strummed when he and Yoko first sang "Give Peace A Chance."

Q: What happens when children come to see the Beatles exhibit?

Rutledge-Borger: One of the many wonderful things about the Beatles legacy is when I see children viewing our memorabilia and listening to the Beatles music. They often know all the words to the songs they are hearing. They know who Paul McCartney is and who John was. It's their real appreciation of the music that I listened to when I was a kid. You know that it's not necessarily imposed on them by their parents. These kids just love it. You see the delight in everybody's face, whether the little ones or the oldsters, like me."

Q: What about the reactions of major rock artists who visit the Rock Hall?

Rutledge-Borger: They're all Beatles fans and are fascinated by the exhibit. There's this universal appeal. No matter what the genre, every rock artist I talk with takes it back to the Beatles. The band's impact on rock music can't be overstated. It was such a sea change. What I find interesting is that they were basically re-doing American music. They created their version of rhythm and blues and sent it back to us.

Lennon's 'tape delayed' Mellotron keyboard

George Harrison produced Jackie Lomax's first Apple Records album

LIVERPOOL SOUL SINGER JACKIE LOMAX

In 2013, I drove to Ojai, California, to track down a rumor. I'd heard there was a Liverpool singer living nearby with ties to the Beatles. After walking the length of the town's covered walkway, I struck up a conversation at a British import shop. That's all it took. The owner said the musician I was looking for was singer Jackie Lomax. He'd been living in Ojai for over twenty years.

Overhearing our conversation, a local bar keeper offered to pass along my phone number. Sure enough, Jackie called me the next day. Two weeks later I was sitting in Lomax's rustic bungalow talking about his remarkable music career. Electric guitar cases and vintage tube amplifiers were strewn about the living room, and black and white photographs taken by early Beatles photographer Astrid Kirchherr lined the walls. Thick brown hair fell across Jackie's shoulders, and he shook hands with fingers that stretched four guitar frets.

Lomax grew up across Liverpool's River Mersey in Wallasey, England. The river's name came to define the Mersey beat sound. It merged Detroit soul and Doo-Wop harmonies with a solid backbeat. In 1962, Lomax became a member of The Undertakers band. They often played on the same bill as the Beatles at The Cavern Club and later in Hamburg, Germany.

Lomax poured a Guinness stout, and I turned on the tape recorder.

Jackie Lomax 2013

Q: What led to you becoming an Apple Records recording artist?

Jackie Lomax: I was signed by the Beatles in 1967 as a songwriter and was working in London for Apple Publishing. That's where George Harrison first heard a couple of my songs. I thought I was writing tunes for other people. He said 'I really like your stuff. Would you like to make an album? I'll produce it.' Inside I was like saying, 'Wow!' But coming from Liverpool, I was kind of casual and low key. I said, 'Yeah, George, that's a really good idea.' It was a great thing, an exhilarating time for me.

Q: In 1968 you released George Harrison's song "Sour Milk Sea." What was that recording session like?

Lomax: It's an amazing rock track. I remember being in the studio and thinking, this sounds like a great instrumental. Well, it's got Eric Clapton blowing great blues licks all over it. He was really slow-hand fast. They brought in Nicky Hopkins on piano. Harrison played guitar and McCartney overdubbed his bass part from the control room. The session was fascinating. It kept going on and on for twelve hours. Before I laid down the lead vocal they brought in flowers, cookies and sandwiches. I remember bringing tea to Ringo in his drum box.

Q: How did you become The Undertakers' lead vocalist?

Lomax: I jumped to The Undertakers when I was seventeen. They had a squirrely bassist and were looking for someone new. I didn't own a bass guitar but the group did, so they let me pay it off. The Undertakers' vocalist used to pick fights with the audience. He was losing us gigs so he had to go.

I said I had a song or two. When they heard my Little Richard cover they said, 'Let's go!' That's how I became the band's lead singer.

Q: What was the scene like in Liverpool and Hamburg in the early 1960s?

Lomax: It was very exciting but really chaotic. Don't tell me that anybody could organize a show with ten bands on it. Little Richard was top of the bill, the Beatles were second and then came groups like the Big Three and my band, The Undertakers. There were only about eight or nine bands in Liverpool at first, not the hundreds of groups you heard about later. In them days we were all in it together. If you blew a speaker, the supporting band would pull in one of theirs and say 'try this one.' We followed The Beatles to Hamburg about a year after they went. It was like being thrown into a Fellini movie.

Q: Did you ever hear your set list being played as you waited backstage?

Lomax: I think John Lennon and I had the same taste for a song. We'd pick the same ones. We didn't know it, but the Beatles did a version of Smokey Robinson's "You Really Got A Hold On Me." We practiced that song for a Cavern show. We walked in and they're playing it. 'Oh well, scrap that one!' "Mr. Moonlight" was another one. It happened too many times.

Q: Did other bands attempt to copy the songs The Undertakers performed?

Lomax: The Hollies tried, but they couldn't figure out where our material came from. They were from Manchester, about 40 miles away. They'd sit in the front row at the Cavern for our show. It was packed to the walls. They were the only ones down front with pads trying to write the words down as I was singing 'em. I gave a nod to the sax player who was a bit of jokester. Then I sang every wrong word I could think of. They wrote them down. When we saw them play in Manchester, they sang our songs — with the wrong words in 'em. We all fell on the floor laughing.

Q: How did you develop your voice?

Lomax: Liverpool seemed to have a lot of high singing bass players. There was Paul McCartney who was very popular and handsome and getting all the chicks. So these other bass players who never thought of singing said, 'I think I can do that.' I was known for my high voice and screams like soul singer James Brown. I never had that raw laryngitis style of Joe Crocker or Rod Stewart. I wanted to sound blacker. I belted it out, but with a more bell-like tone.

Q: What's your view of the Beatles musical legacy?

Lomax: The Beatles influenced every act. Every group ever since uses their harmonies and the slick stuff George Harrison played. They all got it from them. Led Zeppelin was different, but they even got riffs from the Beatles. I was there and saw it. For me, recording with the Beatles was the pinnacle. It was like being on top of the world, but it was a brief thing.

Early 1960's poster from
Hamburg, Germany concert.

MEMORIES

The pursuit of memories is an elusive enterprise. Seeing a Beatle up-close was a fantasy and drinking a pint in Liverpool's Cavern Club was a distant mirage. Both my daydreams came true. I photographed Sir Paul McCartney and Sir Ringo Starr at separate events in 2012–13 and two years later followed the Beatles footsteps through London into Liverpool's famous nightclub. Here are seven kaleidoscopes to peer through. They're Beatles souvenirs; postcards mailed from near and afar.

Ringo Starr 2013

Starr at his LA Grammy Museum Press Conference

STARR POWER

The young American Beatles fan was devastated. Her mother had refused to let her attend the band's 1964 Hollywood Bowl concert. All the thirteen-year-old could do was walk outside and breathe deeply hoping to share the same air with her idol Ringo Starr.

Fifty years later, I interviewed the teenage Beatlemaniac for my newspaper music column. Laurie raved about her summer love affair with the Beatles. I remembered her tale while driving to the opening of Ringo Starr's 2013 Los Angeles

Grammy Museum exhibition. The highlight of the morning's press conference was an appearance by the legendary drummer.

Ringo took the stage with a beaming smile. His hair and beard were closely cropped. He wore stylish shaded glasses and sported a hip earring pin. Always upbeat and witty, the ultra-slim Starr looked hale and healthy. After being introduced by the museum's executive director Bob Santelli, Ringo stood to take questions.

Q: Who was your musical idol?

Ringo Starr: Lightnin' Hopkins! You know life is weird. When I was eighteen years old, I went to the American consulate in Liverpool because I wanted to move to Houston, Texas because Lightnin' was from there. We (Ringo and friends) were working factory jobs in Liverpool at the time. They gave us all these forms so we filled them out and handed them in. Then they gave us more forms. Well, we were young and didn't follow up. Life takes a strange path.

Then Starr turned and pointed at me. I asked him about the band's storied heritage.

Q: What are your thoughts about the musical legacy you helped create?

Ringo Starr: Yeah, I love it! (laughter) I do love it because I'm really proud of the music we made. It took a while but we were very serious players and the results are still being played today. That's what's great. It's still going on. How great is that, you know? The memories I have of those days, I'd like to say every minute was great. It wasn't. But overall the emotion was great. We worked hard. We only wanted to be musicians. We didn't sort of sit around and say, let's be famous. We said, let's be musicians. And as you all know, unless you're from another planet, the Beatles became very famous. That was part of it — but the music was the most important thing we did.

Sneak Preview

"Ringo: Peace and Love" was the first major exhibition of memorabilia from Starr's large collection. The Grammy Museum display included the pink military-style costume Ringo wore on the cover of *Sgt. Pepper*, his original black leather Beatle Boots and the Ludwig Oyster Pearl drum kit he played on the Ed Sullivan Show.

Starr's drum kit at the LA Grammy Museum

The exhibition also showed a seventeen minute retrospective film of Starr's career, including Paul McCartney's 2010 rocking performance of "Birthday" with Starr playing drums. Behind a glass case were Ringo's hand-written lyrics to his first original song, "Don't Pass Me By," which appeared on the band's *White Album*.

Starr's off-the-cuff remarks became the titles of Beatles songs including, "A Hard Day's Night" and "Tomorrow Never Knows." They're called malapropisms. The term comes from a 1775 play entitled *The Rivals*. In the comedy, Mrs. Malaprop repeatedly and humorously confuses words with similar sounds and meanings.

Here are five of Ringo Starr's mixed-up gems:

From 1964 British music television show Ready Steady Go:

Q: "Are you a mod or a rocker?"

Ringo: "No, I'm a mocker."

"I like Beethoven, especially the poems."

Ringo on the band's 1964 US Tour: "So this is America. They must be out of their minds."

"I'm not going to say anything–'cause nobody believes me when I do."

"I'd like to end up–sort of–unforgettable."

As Ringo left the Grammy Museum that day, he paused next to an exhibition of his e-book *Photograph*. It spotlights Starr's previously unpublished early Beatles photos. Then it was time to go. He flashed his trademark peace sign, smiled and waved goodbye. Tucked into a waiting limo, Starr escaped into LA's bright sunshine.[2]

---

2   *On 3-20-18 Ringo Starr was knighted by Prince William, Duke of Cambridge, at Buckingham Palace.*

Ringo Starr's Anello & Davide "Beatle boots"

SIR PAUL MCCARTNEY IN HOLLYWOOD

February 9, 2012

When I learned that Paul McCartney was to be enshrined on Hollywood's Walk of Fame, I knew I had to be there. I'd never seen him in person. I was on the road before sunrise for the ninety-mile drive to Hollywood. The ceremony was to take place at 2 p.m. in front of the Capitol Records building. I figured leaving early would provide me with a good spot to photograph McCartney. All four Beatles received their Member of the Most Excellent Member of the British Empire (MBE) medals in 1965 and Sir Paul McCartney was knighted in 1996 by Queen Elizabeth. Because of scheduling problems, his three bandmates had received their Hollywood Stars before McCartney.

I pulled up at 7 a.m. and was shocked to see 200 fans already in line. So much for beating the crowd. The early arrivers held hand-made placards and oversized Beatles photos, and one guy had a replica Hofner guitar swung over his shoulder. Over the next seven hours our band of fans became 2,000 strong. The long line snaked around the corner and down the street. We settled in for a long wait but soon were sharing concert stories and making food runs.

McCartney spoke to 2,000
fans in Hollywood.

Paul McCartney before the Hollywood Walk Ceremony

Suddenly it was time. The security team dropped the rope line and the bulging crowd poured into the street. I ran toward the front but still found myself ten yards from the stage. Then McCartney stepped into our view. The excited surge pushed me five feet forward. That clamorous, crazy moment was breathtaking-seconds you always remember. Sir Paul stepped forward and waved to the excited, appreciative crowd.

Rock musician Neil Young was on hand to introduce McCartney. He said he'd learned to play the Beatles music as a high school musician. "No one could figure out what Paul was doing on bass. He played it in a way no one had ever played the instrument before," he said. Young continued: "I want to tell you that as a musician and songwriter, Paul McCartney's craft is art. He's truly at the top of his game, just like Charlie Chaplin was a great actor, but it's the soul of Paul's music that makes me feel so good."

Then it was McCartney's turn. The crowd hung on his words. "Back in the day, in Liverpool, when we were listening to Buddy Holly, I never thought there would be a day I would get my star on the Walk of Fame," McCartney smiled. He credited his bandmates' contributions and the musical legacy they created together. No notes or speech, just simple and straightforward.

Was it worth the great wait? For a Beatles fan, it doesn't get any better.

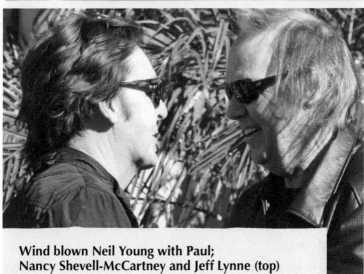

**Wind blown Neil Young with Paul;
Nancy Shevell-McCartney and Jeff Lynne (top)**

Browsing at the Fest's Marketplace

BEATLES CONCLAVE

October 10-12, 2014

It had been fourteen years since Los Angeles hosted a *Fest For Beatles Fans*. The fan conclave was held at Marriott's modern LAX Airport Hotel. I bought a three-day pass to the event based on the number of Beatles-era artists and special guests scheduled to appear. I wasn't disappointed.

John Lennon's sister, Julia Baird, posed for photos and signed autographs in the Fest's large marketplace. Paul McCartney's sister, Ruth, chatted with fans and sold her own brand of 'McCartney Tea.' Beatles promoter Bob Eubanks held court on the main thoroughfare next to Liverpool singer Billy J. Kramer.

After screening her 2013 documentary film, "*Good Ol'Freda*," Beatles Fan Club Secretary Freda Kelly was mobbed by affectionate admirers. Kelly was a seventeen-year-old Liverpool typist when Beatles manager Brian Epstein hired her as his personal secretary. She ran the band's Fan Club until 1971.

Stars Align

Throughout the Fest there were panel discussions and presentations from dozens of Beatles authors, some of whom had flown in from England. I filed their business cards away, day-dreaming about a trip to Liverpool.

Walking through the hotel's main hall, I bumped into Wings guitarists Denny Laine and Laurence Juber and drummer Denny Seiwell. On Friday night all three former members of McCartney's band performed together, accompanied by talented East Coast Beatles tribute band Liverpool.

Badfinger lead guitarist Joey Molland was also on hand to play his hits, including "Baby Blue" and "No Matter What." On Saturday night, Billy J. Kramer reprised his 1963 No.1 UK Hit "Bad To Me," which was written by John Lennon. The most startling moment was Kramer's revelation that he turned down Paul McCartney's ballad "Yesterday." He painfully remembered saying to Paul, "Don't you have a rock and roll song?"

Peter Asher performs at the 2014 Fest For Beatles Fans

Billy J. Kramer with the Beatles

Fab Finale

On Sunday morning the Fest's Master of Ceremonies, Chris Carter, broadcast his "Breakfast With The Beatles" radio show live from the Marriott. The weekend's final concert was singer Peter Asher's two-hour showcase, "Musical Memoir of The '60s and Beyond." His multi-media performance was accented with hits "World Without Love," "I Go To Pieces," "Lady Godiva" and "Woman."

Asher's finale featured a (video screen) duet with his former musical partner who died in 2009. The pairing was a fitting bookend for the weekend celebration. At my last Beatles convention in 2001, I had secured the autograph of Gordon Waller, the other half of Asher's duo, Peter & Gordon.

I left the Fest with a smile. Under my arm were a scarce 1963 Beatles poster, a signed copy of Freda Kelly's documentary, a colorful 1964 Ringo Starr fan magazine and an autographed photo of singer Billy J. Kramer with the Beatles. Not a bad haul for about $75.00.

Formal entrance to London's Royal Albert Hall

Inside Albert Hall in 2015

POSTCARDS FROM ENGLAND

Dreams can gnaw at you and sometimes they come true. In 2015 I flew to England to trace the Beatles' footsteps. On my first day in London I toured Royal Albert Hall.

The horseshoe-shaped, multi-tiered concert hall first opened in 1871 and seats over 5,000 people. Over 325 concerts are held there each year. We sat one stall away from the Queen's Box as our tour guide explained the Hall's storied history. The Beatles performed at Albert Hall twice in 1963 and John Lennon referenced the concert venue with a psychedelic lyric in the Beatles song "A Day in the Life."

Next, I viewed the British Library's collection of original Beatles songs. The band's official biographer, Hunter Davis, often picked up lyric scraps at the band's EMI recording sessions and donated them to the museum's archives. The words to Beatles songs "Help," "Yesterday," "Ticket To Ride," "Michele" and "I Want To Hold Your Hand" are on display in a glass case near Shakespeare's First Folio published in 1623. Davis also gave the British Library several letters written by John Lennon and handwritten lyrics to three of his songs, "Strawberry Fields Forever," "She Said She Said" and "In My Life."

That afternoon I embarked on the first of two small-group Beatles walking tours. The guide's brisk pace allowed us to visit several dozen sites including Ringo's former Montagu Square flat. It's where Lennon and wife Yoko posed naked for the cover of their *Two Virgins* album. In 1966 Jimi Hendrix wrote "The Wind Cries Mary" in the basement's quarters. Paul McCartney had previously used the space as a demo recording studio.

Around the corner from MPL Communications (McCartney Productions Ltd.) is Trident Studios, located on narrow St. Anne's Court. The Beatles recorded "Hey Jude" there and *White Album* tracks including "Savoy Truffle," "Dear Prudence" and "Martha My Dear." After a short stroll, we paused in front of the Beatles former Apple Records offices on Savile Row. It was the location of their legendary 1969 rooftop concert.

Both tours ended at the St. John's Wood Tube station, a two-block shuffle to Abbey Road Studios and the famous zebra-striped crosswalk. The Beatles used it for their 1969 album cover. Paul McCartney's house on Cavendish Avenue is nearby. His three-story Victorian terraced home sits behind a high wooden gate. The street was quiet when I walked by that afternoon, but in the mid-'60s fans regularly gathered out front. McCartney wrote "She Came In Through the Bathroom Window" after a Beatles groupie used a ladder to slip into his bedroom.

McCartney's home in St. John's Wood, London 2015

TWENTY-FOUR HOURS IN LIVERPOOL: TRIP JOURNAL

11:05 p.m.: After three revealing days in London I arrived at Liverpool's Lime Street Station. The journey took just over two hours on Virgin's fast train. A black cab deposited me at The Jury's Inn, situated on Liverpool's waterfront. After checking in, I walked to nearby Albert Docks and gazed across the River Mersey.

7:30 a.m.: Following a full English breakfast including bangers, baked beans and tomatoes, I strolled to the nearby Beatles Story Museum. The rambling exhibition includes George Martin's hand-written studio notes and the white piano John Lennon played in his "Imagine" music video. I was watching the clock because I'd pre-booked three tours that day, including a Magical Mystery Bus ramble through Liverpool.

9:15 a.m.: The coach guide spoke with a thick Scouse Liverpool accent. He said it was producer Martin who suggested Lennon and McCartney each write a song about their childhood memories. As "Penny Lane" played in the background, we drove by the places McCartney sang about including the bank, the barber shop, the round-about and nearby fire station. It was startling to realize the song's locales were always real and still exist.

11:05 a.m.: I had my photo snapped on Penny Lane and in front of the former Salvation Army orphanage that inspired Lennon's "Strawberry Fields Forever." His childhood home is located adjacent to the former institution. Standing next to its famous red iron gates, I felt as if I'd stepped inside Lennon's art rock opus. Lennon often wrote in the first person. His lyrics to "A Day in the Life" were inspired by a British newspaper story, and the images in "Being for the Benefit of Mr. Kite!"were crafted from a circus poster.

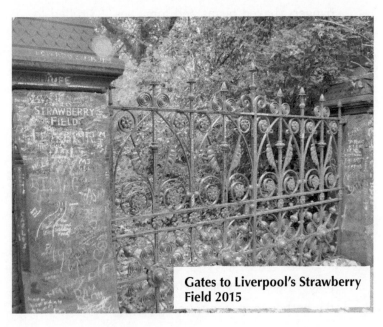

Gates to Liverpool's Strawberry Field 2015

1:15 p.m.: I sat at a lunch counter in downtown Liverpool and enjoyed an order of fish & chips splashed with vinegar. The city's center is thriving and truly frenetic at lunchtime. I got turned around in its warren of narrow streets and had to run six blocks to meet the National Trust van.

1:30p.m.: When I arrived at the pickup point, I realized I was the only person booked on tours of both Lennon's and McCartney's childhood/teenage homes. What good luck! The driver invited me to sit up front, and we struck up a conversation. He said that Yoko Ono purchased Lennon's Mendips home in 2002 for 150,000 pounds ($291,000 US) and donated it to the National Trust. McCartney's home was purchased by the Trust from a subsequent owner in 1995. Both houses have been restored to their original condition with period furnishings and personal items donated from Lennon's estate and McCartney's family.

2:00 p.m.: The first stop was 20 Forthlin Road where McCartney lived during his teens. I was met by a friendly guide who asked me not to take photographs inside. The modest two-story brick row home has a shared garden and coal shed out back. The only bathroom is upstairs. John, Paul and George lived within a five-mile radius but Ringo was raised further away, in the rough-and-tumble Dingle neighborhood. Harrison and Lennon often hung out at McCartney's place. The band's first single, "Love Me Do," was written there.

Author in front of McCartney's National Trust home

2:15 p.m.: What a moment — stepping through the front door into McCartney's small, bright living room. It's where Paul penned pulsing rocker "I Saw Her Standing There" and early ballad "I'll Follow The Sun." When McCartney was sixteen, he wrote the melody to "When I'm Sixty-Four" on the family piano. An upright still stands against the room's far wall.

McCartney grew up in a musical family. Brother Mike's drums were kept in a small dining room off the kitchen. Paul's dad led his extended family in group sing alongs. Harmony was an art form in the McCartney home. I could almost hear their joined voices.

3:30 p.m.: Then we were off to John Lennon's home. He lived with his Aunt Mimi for eighteen years on leafy Menlove Ave. McCartney would often ride his bike over to play guitar. Lennon wrote "Please Please Me" in his upstairs bedroom. Its descending melody/harmony line changed pop music forever.

I looked through a copy Lennon's British passport, which showed the band's worldwide travels, including their trips to Australia, India and the Philippines. There were headphones on both Lennon's and McCartney's bed frames. Each was connected by a long wire to downstairs radio sets. Both teens would listen to Radio Luxembourg's rock music broadcasts far into the night.

5:45 p.m.: The National Trust driver dropped me at my dockside hotel. After a chicken curry dinner, I walked six blocks to Liverpool's Cavern Club at 10 Mathew Street. The legendary nightclub first opened in 1957 but was closed in 1973 during the construction of an underground Tube line. It reopened nearby in 1984 using the Cavern's original blueprints and bricks.

The Cavern featured Jazz in 1957

8:30 p.m.: You feel the pulsing beat as you descend twenty-eight steps from the street into the cellar nightclub. There's a compact bar at the bottom of the staircase with memorabilia displays and merchandise cases lining the walls. The club's backline gear includes a black pearl Ludwig drum set and two classic Vox amplifiers. A live band was playing 60s covers that night. As their riffs bounced off the stone archways, I could almost feel the Beatles' presence. From 1961–63, they performed at the club nearly 300 times.

10:55p.m.: To top off the night, I decided to have a pint at Grapes just down Mathew Street. The Beatles used to hangout at the pub between their Cavern Club sets. There's a 1963 photo on the wall showing the band relaxing in their favorite booth. After my drink, it was time to go and sleep fast. The next day I was on the 7 a.m. train back to London and then home to the States.

My journey through London and Liverpool continues to resonate. Was I really there? I imagine so, but it seems like a dream.

The Beatles first Cavern Club performance was Feb 9th, 1961

MEETING A BEATLE

I photographed Sir Paul McCartney at his 2012 Hollywood Walk of Fame instillation and asked Ringo Starr a question at his 2013 Los Angeles Grammy Museum press conference, but I hadn't actually *met* a Beatle. My luck was about to change. After the publication of *Postcards From Liverpool*, I was invited to speak at the 2018 San Diego Beatles Fair. I decided the timing was right to revisit Yoko Ono's 60's poetry because she had been awarded co-writing credit for John Lennon's greatest solo recording "Imagine" by the National Music Publishers Association.

Other than Ms. Ono, the only member of the Beatles' inner circle to receive less recognition for the band's success, was their longest-tenured original percussionist. He was unceremoniously drummed out of the group on August 16, 1962 after playing hundreds of shows in Hamburg's nightclubs and Northern England venues, including Liverpool's Cavern Club.

This was the fate of drummer Pete Best. He was a Beatle for 2 years. Manager Brian Epstein gave him the bad news after he'd recorded both the Beatles Decca Records demos and the A & B sides of their first EMI 45rpm record "Love Me Do" and "P.S. I Love You." The Liverpool band Mr. Best joined after being sacked (Lee Curtis and the All-Stars) was managed by a friend of Brian Epstein and later signed by Decca Records, the London label that had rejected the Beatles.

Liverpool's reaction to Mr. Best's dismissal was swift and brutal. Front row Cavern Club fans held up newspapers during the Beatles sets to express their outrage. George Harrison was headbutted by a Teddy Boy type inside the Cavern Club. Fan reaction lingered but was short lived. Less than a year later the Beatles played their final Cavern Club show, the band's first album "Please Please Me" became a No.1 UK Hit and their new single "From Me To You" reached the top of the English charts.

Pete Best, 76, was the headline guest for the 2018 San Diego Beatles Fair. His trap set was flown in from Liverpool to Queen Bee's Arts & Cultural Center located in the hip North Park section of the city. The two-day event featured an onstage interview with Mr. Best followed by a live performance by the legendary drummer. I found a prime seat three rows from the front as Best regaled the crowd with an uproarious, hour long, off-the-cuff interview. He's a master storyteller who mixes humorous anecdotes and revealing Beatles tales into his Liverpool cocktail. During the audience Q&A, I asked him which songs he sang with the Beatles in Hamburg and Liverpool. He smiled, smirked and quipped, "As few as possible." Then he quickly added, "There were a couple I sang, 'Matchbox,' and 'Peppermint Twist' but none of them were ever recorded."

Drummer Pete Best regaled the San Diego crowd.

Although Mr. Best's new group (The All-Stars) twice shared Liverpool stages with the Beatles, he never spoke to any member of the band after his dismissal. Over the last fifty years, both George Harrison and Paul McCartney said they shouldn't have left Mr. Best's firing solely to their manager, but they worried a fist fight would break out if they were present. None of the Beatles ever second guessed their decision to hire Ringo Starr. One bright spot for Mr. Best was the release of the 1995 Beatles Anthology Video/CD set. He implied he'd been well paid for the Anthology project which featured his drumming on six tracks.

Near the end of his San Diego interview, Mr. Best was asked to describe each of the Beatles members in just one word. He paused for dramatic effect and jumped into the fire. "Lennon: Genius. McCartney: Genius. Harrison: Genius. Here's a bonus for you, Sutcliff: Genius." Someone shouted, "How about you?" "Genius," he immediately deadpanned. There was only one Beatle left. Mr. Best scanned the audience and slyly stated: "Starr: Drummer." And that was it. Old wounds can still sting.

A front row fan exclaimed that Pete Best possessed "history's most famous right foot." He suggested that Mr. Best's use of the bass drum propelled the Beatles Merseybeat sound and powered their early arrangements. The band's German handlers urged the Beatles to "make a show" to lure new customers off the street. Because Mr. Best's drums weren't mic'd in Hamburg, he responded by doubling up his snare shots and bass drum rhythms. Pete Best's drumming style was named the Atom Beat for its four on the floor, thundering bass drum patterns and tumbling tom-tom fills.

Pete Best's sticks still snap!

After returning from their marathon 1960–61 Hamburg gigs, the Beatles became Liverpool's top band. Mr. Best said one of the reasons for their success was that each night the

German police would throw underage teenagers out of city's kinky nightclubs. "We had to adapt to a new audience and added some calmer songs and original material for the older crowd. We took those songs back to Liverpool." Mr. Best revealed that he's involved in a new business venture, the construction of a Beatles Museum on Liverpool's Mathew Street near The Cavern Club.

We eagerly awaited the stage curtains to open. It was time to hear Mr. Best perform. With his brother Roag playing next to him on a second drum set and accompanied by San Diego rock legends the Falling Doves, Pete Best ripped through a six song set including, "Money," "Mr. Postman," "Slow Down," "Rock 'n Roll Music," "I Saw Her Standing There" and an extended version of "Twist and Shout." After the show ended, Mr. Best disappeared into a sea of cell phone holding fans. The line to secure his autograph was forty deep.

Day two of the San Diego Beatles Fair featured spot-on tribute artists The Baja Bugs and the talented Dave Humphries Band, whose Scottish lead singer dropped off a demo tape at London's Apple Records but never got a reply. During the presenter's panel, I commented that Yoko Ono was a trained classical pianist who often contributed to her husband's music. She wasn't credited for the song "Give Peace A Chance," although John Lennon later said they wrote it together on their honeymoon. Listening to his wife perform Beethoven's "Moonlight Sonata," Mr. Lennon asked Yoko if she could play the score backwards. Lennon then used Beethoven's chord forms to craft the song "Because," which is found on the band's *Abbey Road* album. It's a vocal masterpiece, featuring tri-part harmony blended in perfect parallel thirds. I noted that Ms. Ono's re-issued book of poetry entitled "Grapefruit" contains the word "imagine" 12 times in her poems, and her two-line word painting, Cloud Piece, is found in very small print, in the lower left hand corner, on the back cover of John Lennon's "Imagine" album. Mr. Lennon said his most recognized solo recording would not have been written or emerged without his wife's poetry.

Zak Nilsson, the son of legendary rock musician Harry Nilsson, was at the Beatles fair collecting signatures for his father to be inducted into the Rock & Roll Hall of Fame. A noteworthy endeavor! The day's unexpected musical highlight was an appearance by Ringo Starr look-alike Ringer Star. His spot-on stage moves and engaging performance of Mr. Starr's hits brought cheers from the tuned-in crowd.

The Beatles performed in San Diego, CA just once on August 28, 1965 at Balboa Stadium. Reserved seats were priced from $3.50 to $5.50 USD. Incredibly, the concert wasn't a complete sell out because two feuding rock radio stations caused problems with ticket distribution. The Beatles didn't miss a beat and received $50,000 for their 12-song, 35-minute long show. Band members ate Kentucky

Fried Chicken backstage (reportedly the Beatles favorite American food), while four warm-up acts entertained the 17,000-plus fans in attendance. They included Cannibal and the Headhunters, and soul singer Brenda Holloway, who co-wrote the song "You Made Me So Very Happy" which in 1969 rose to No.2 on the Billboard Singles Chart for band Blood, Sweat & Tears. Also on the bill were the Brian Epstein-managed group Sound Incorporated and saxophone great King Curtis and the Kingpins.

San Diego Beatles historian Steve Thorn said that all hell broke loose after the concert ended. "Fans burst through the stadium's security barriers and John Lennon and Paul McCartney were seen running across the football field toward their tour bus. Ringo Starr appeared bemused by the chaos until George Harrison pulled him out of harm's way," Thorn said. "As if that weren't enough, the Beatles bus broke down in front of a funeral home outside Balboa Stadium," Thorn laughed. "With fans gathering, manager Epstein had to order limousines rescue the band and drive them to Los Angeles for their next show at the Hollywood Bowl."

That afternoon, Mr. Best received a proclamation from the San Diego City Council decreeing that March 31, 2018 was Pete Best Day. With typical Liverpudlian humor, the drummer sheepishly asked the councilman, "I was just wondering, will there be a Pete Best Day next year?" Then with plaque in hand he ducked off stage. As I edged my way into the crowded backstage green room, I spied Mr. Best who was posing for photographs. This was my chance to meet a Beatle.

The famed drummer laughed as I handed him a copy of my book. "Ah, another one!" he quipped. "Thanks, I'll have a look," he smiled. We chatted a bit about Liverpool's haunts and his new endeavors before taking an unforgettable photo. Is there a meet up in my future with Paul McCartney, Ringo Starr or Yoko Ono? Maybe my moment with Mr. Best underlines a universal axiom. If destiny is forged by opportunities with uncertain outcomes, just about anything that can happen, will.

Author Brickley meets drummer Pete Best

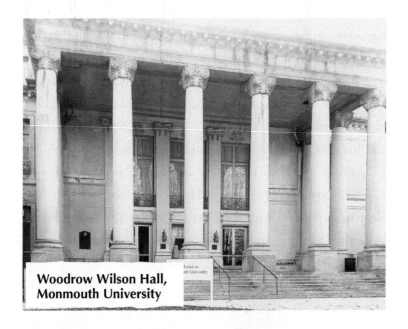

**Woodrow Wilson Hall,
Monmouth University**

THE WHITE ALBUM: AN INTERNATIONAL SYMPOSIUM

November 8th–11th 2018: Monmouth University

Drawing over 350 Beatles scholars, authors and enthusiasts to an academic focused Beatles event is no easy task. Monmouth University's White Album International Symposium eclipsed my expectations. Its focus was the 50th Anniversary of the Beatles White Album and the release of the band's remixed and remastered tracks, including the original "Esher Demos," alternate cuts, outtakes and recording studio chatter. The Beatles original 1968 LP is a tapestry of sound with finger picked ballads, raunchy blues, country riffs and plenty of scorching rock 'n' roll. The double LP's thirty tracks feature Music Hall sing-alongs, "Revolution #9's" experimental tape-looped effects and Ringo Starr's first original song. It's a dizzying, wondrous, ageless album.

The guiding light behind the International Symposium was Monmouth University Dean/Professor and Beatles author, Ken Womack. He presented a fascinating web of White Album focused lectures, renowned speakers and musicians who performed selections from the celebrated Beatles LP. Each morning and afternoon we chose from a stimulating buffet of Beatles presentations. I met scholars and Beatles fans from Finland, Canada, Australia and across the USA. Here are selected highlights of the Symposium's lectures and special events that I attended.

Day One/Thursday Ashbury Park Walking Tour

I flew into Newark, NJ from Los Angeles the night before, and on Thursday morning drove toward campus under scarlet oaks, and sugar maple trees performing their brilliant change of color. I'd never visited Monmouth University before and was unaware it's located less than five miles from the Jersey Shore. The reason I came east a day early was to tour the hangouts of a local rock superstar.

Monmouth University is home to the *Bruce Springsteen Archives* which is the official repository of Springsteen's written works, photographs, periodicals and artifacts. The collection comprises nearly 35,000 items from 47 countries ranging from books and concert memorabilia to articles and promotional materials.

Singer/Songwriter Bruce Springsteen put Ashbury Park on the map. He formed his E Street Band with local musicians, including saxophonist Clarence Clemons and guitarist Steve Van Zandt. We strolled down shore's famous wooden Boardwalk and visited the clubs and venues where Springsteen played including The Wonder Bar, The Paramount Theater and Convention Hall (Elvis Costello performed there night before). We stopped by the former Upstage Club where The Boss began in 1969 and were warmly greeted at Springsteen photographer Danny Clinch's studio.

Ashbury Park's Stone Pony Nightclub.

Inside The Stone Pony.

The tour's last stop was The Stone Pony which opened in 1974 and helped jump start Springsteen's career. The Boss also met his wife Patti Scalia in the club's back bar. The Pony is ranked just behind Liverpool's Cavern Club as the world's most famous rock club. Springsteen hasn't played in Ashbury Park for years but he was spotted in 2018 hanging out at the Wonder Bar. The two hour Springsteen tour cost $35 and was offered as an add-on to the conference schedule.

The Weeklings Concert

Monmouth University's Pollak Theater was the setting for *The Weeklings* White Album tribute concert. The show's admission was included in the symposium's registration fee along with almost everything else during the four day event, including lunch and dinner meals with entertainment, films and multi-media lectures.

**The Weeklings perform at Monmouth University,
L to R: Bellia, Merjave, Burtnick, Burger.**

I was struck by bassist Glen Burtnick's musical skills hearing him perform with *The Weeklings*. His command of the bass is so advanced it's as if the instrument plays itself. What I didn't know is that Burtnick was a former member of band *Styx*, played Paul McCartney in the Broadway production of *Beatlemania* and is the current bassist in *The Orchestra*, which is made up of former members of the *Electric Light Orchestra*.

Burtnick was joined by explosive lead guitarist John Merjave, smooth rhythm ace Bob Burger and black-gloved power drummer Joe Bellia. They played deep cuts from the Beatles White Album accompanied by a string quartet on songs including "I Will" & "Julia" and a powerful horn section on cuts "Savoy Truffle" & "Birthday." It was one of those shows that you remember forever and the evening didn't end with "Let It Be's" the last refrain. At midnight there was a White

Album remix listening session, but I was headed back to the Sheraton Hotel anticipating Friday morning's sessions.

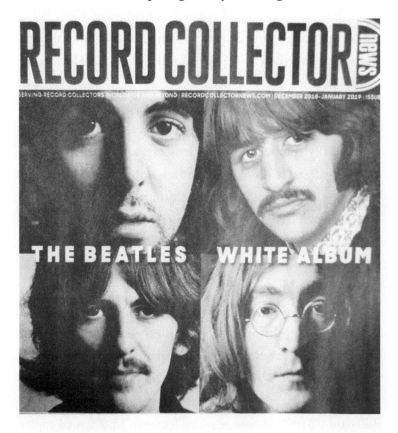

Day Two/Friday

The day's first lecture was titled *Multi-colored Mirrors: Mixing, Modulation, Momentum* which dissected how the Beatles constructed their songs. Beatles wiz Aaron Krerowicz determined that 30% of the Beatles songs have key changes and broke down the eight White Album's songs that modulate keys. The second speaker, Matthew Schneider of High Point University, detailed the Beatles fundamental song progressions and ended his talk with a joke. Q: Mr. Harrison, "How many Beatles does it take to change a light bulb? A: "Four," Harrison quipped, "To show solidarity!" During audience questions Krerowicz responded that key changes in Beatles songs were usually spontaneous decisions rather than pre-planned creations. Beatles scholar Mark Lewisohn (who was seated behind me) agreed stating, "Yes, their songwriting was intuitive."

On Friday afternoon I moderated the symposium panel *"Revival: Repackaging the Beatle*s." Presenters included Lena Stagg, co-host of Beatles podcast "She Said-She Said." Lena introduced the audience to Canadian hip-hop star Drake and explained how Billboard Chart success now differs from the Beatles charted hits of the 1960s. The Beatles White Album spent nine weeks at No.1 on the Billboard 200 Chart (between December 28, 1968 and March 1, 1969) and sold four million copies worldwide. Drake's albums have repeatedly topped the Billboard Charts, but have required less than 75,000 total copies sold, including streaming sales to become No. 1 chart hits.

Up next was professor Jim Von Shilling's presentation titled *"The Beatles vs. The Kinks: 1966–1968."* He selected seven pairs of Beatles and Kinks single records, played key moments from each song, made comparisons and tallied his votes. Amazingly the Kinks came out on top! For my ears they never topped their first raw rock single "You Really Got Me."

L-R: Author Bruce Spizer, Rob Sheffield of Rolling Stone Magazine, Beatles scholar Mark Lewisohn and DJ/moderator Ken Dashow shared their White Album insights.

Day Three/Saturday:

Viewing the Beatles music through the arch of history was the focus of Saturday morning's group discussion, *Revolution: 1968 The White Album in Context*. Panel members discussed how the French student uprising may have influenced John Lennon to write song "Revolution" and commented that the White Album contains many of the band's most lyrically topical tracks, likely influenced by their trip to Rishikesh, India. The free flowing discussion included whether or not one should believe Beatles roadie Mal Evans who said that McCartney wrote song "Blackbird" simply observing a bird singing in Rishikesh. McCartney said that "Blackbird's" lyrics were composed with a social justice overlay.

Another discussion point offered that cult leader Charles Manson completely misinterpreted Beatles song "Helter Skelter," which describes a British carnival ride with a circular slide, not an impending race war. Panel member Kit O'Toole summed up the morning's White Album presentation stating, "It's a timeless album that was a product of its time."

Later that morning, I attended Jude Southerland Kessler's presentation titled *Lennon's White: A Darker Shade of Pale*. She is the author of four factually-researched narrative books on the life of John Lennon and expects to write five more volumes to complete her series. Kessler is also the co-host of podcast *She-Said, She-Said* and revealed that Lennon was a voracious reader who devoured Balzac's books by the time he was eight. After Lennon's Uncle George died of cirrhosis of the liver, John's mother Julia returned to his life and taught him to play the banjo and guitar. She told him he was destined to become a great performer and he believed her. Kessler said that Yoko Ono tirelessly pursued Lennon, but he kept Ono's book "Grapefruit" on his night stand while he was married to Cynthia. Lennon later remarked that Ono reminded him of his mother.

The premier event of the International Symposium was Saturday night's multi-media presentation by Mark Lewisohn, the acknowledged world authority on the Beatles. His lecture was titled: *Double Lives: Between the Beatles Grooves.* Lewisohn cleverly designed his presentation as a video notebook and selected audio, video and photographic highlights of the band that occurred before and during the making of the White Album, including the following:

- Britain's *New Musical Express* newspaper column *From You To Us* was the inspiration for the Beatles No. 1 British 1963 Hit single, "From Me To You." It also reached the top spot on the USA Billboard singles chart in 1964.
- In 1967 John Lennon bought *Dornish Island* located in Clew Bay/County Mayo, Ireland for 1700 British pounds (about $4,800 US), but only visited it once. He invited a group of hippies to establish a commune there in 1970. After Lennon's murder in 1980 Yoko Ono sold Dornish for nearly 30,000 British pounds and donated the proceeds to an Irish orphanage.
- In 1968 Italian Film Director Franco Zeffirelli met with Paul McCartney and asked him to star in his film *Romeo & Juliet,* opposite actress Olivia Hussey, but McCartney turned down the role.
- In 1968 all four Beatles chipped in for a wedding gift for their former road manager Neil Aspinall. They bought him a townhouse in London's tony Knightsbridge district.

- Mark Lewisohn exclaimed that the Paul McCartney penned Beatles song, "Penny Lane" is the greatest pop single issued by anyone, at any time.

Day Four/Sunday:

Talk More Talk panel with Beatles producer Chris Thomas (3rd from right)

The Symposium's *Talk More Talk: The Beatles Solo Year*'s podcast special guest was Beatles producer Chris Thomas.

While George Martin was on a two week vacation, Thomas produced seven tracks on the band's 1968 White Album including *"Birthday," "Helter Skelter," "Savoy Truffle," "Piggies"* and *"Happiness Is A Warm Gun."* Thomas also performed on several Beatles tracks and penned "Savoy Truffle's" driving saxophone arrangement. The Talk More Talk podcast was broadcast live on Facebook.com and co-hosted by Beatles experts Ken Womack, Kit O'Toole, Ken Michaels and Tom Hunyady.

Discussing his musical influences, Thomas cited Buddy Holly's use of echo repeat and said record producer Phil Spector was his "absolute idol." The 21-year-old Thomas said his first day in Abbey Road Studios was rough because George Martin didn't leave him any production notes. "I realized that if I didn't step up I wouldn't get invited back. I didn't know anything technical at first because I was at EMI as a musician."

After his work with the Beatles, Thomas produced albums for *The Pretenders*, *Pink Floyd*, *Badfinger*, *Roxy Music*, *INXS* and the *Sex Pistols*, among others. He responded candidly to Kit O'Toole's question about 2018's remixed White Album. "A remix is like hearing a song from another direction in the room, so it sounds different. For me it destroys the original image which was always the (Beatles) mono version. When you take all the original ingredients out and re-bake it, I find that very strange—it was a finished product," Thomas said. Co-host Ken Womack suggested that remixing may be like questioning an author after they sign off and publish a book, "creating their own mono/stereo original."

Here's a sampling of the Q&A's from the hour-long live podcast:

Q: What did you learn about the producer's role while working with the Beatles?

Thomas: "They welcomed me and I did what they asked me to do! The producer's role is that the record should be better at the end of the day, with your involvement."

Q: Was the band *Wings* a collaborative group or did they only mirror McCartney's vision?

Thomas: "Well, Paul without any question was the person in charge (of *Wings*) and he knew what he wanted most of the time. The musicians brought their own personality--that's how band's work. Paul is the genius, it's extraordinary—he works at a high level all the time. Remember McCartney recorded three original songs "I'm Down," "Yesterday" and "I've Just Seen A Face" in one day (June 14, 1965)."

Q: One of your strengths as a producer is bringing an artist's sound up to date but not detracting from their signature sound. How did you accomplish that during the 1980s working with Elton John?

Thomas: "With Elton I got his original band back together, so it's the musicians that make that (signature) sound more than anything else. You don't get a Mussel Shoals sound without having those guys playing either."

Q: How did you weld together the three sections in Beatles song "Happiness Is A Warm Gun?"

Thomas: "It took two days just to get a backing track because they had to learn all those time changes. You can hear how complicated it is. They played and played to get it better. The band had a real sense of purpose."

Beatles historian Mark Lewisohn was the mystery guest for Sunday's luncheon presentation.

For Sunday's final presentation attendees were invited to bring a piece of Beatles history with them to be discussed by a mystery guest. No one knew who the Beatles expert would be until Beatles scholar Mark Lewisohn stepped to the podium. The first artifact randomly selected belonged to a young man wearing a 'Teddy Boy' Liverpool jacket and black Anello & Davide Beatles boots. He was holding a stunning blonde Rickenbacker electric six string guitar. Mr. Lewisohn correctly identified it as a copy of John Lennon's early 60s stage guitar which Lennon eventually painted black. My number was chosen next and I presented Mr. Lewisohn with a Grand Tour ticket from London's Royal Albert Hall. He easily filled five minutes talking about the Beatles two 1963 performances at Albert Hall, once sharing the marquee with the Rolling Stones.

As Monmouth University's International White Album Symposium came to a close, it was announced that planning has begun for a September 2019 conference at The University of Rochester (New York), to celebrate the 50th anniversary of the *Abbey Road* album. That will be something!

John Lennon's/Yoko Ono's 1968 flat
on Montagu Square in London.

POSTSCRIPTS

After the Beatles broke apart in 1970, each band member recorded new studio albums. Before his murder in 1980, John Lennon had created eleven. George Harrison finished twelve prior to his death in 2001. With 2019's, *What's My Name*, Ringo Starr has produced twenty studio albums. Paul McCartney has released twenty-five albums with 2018's *Egypt Station*. Here's a deep look at just one of the sixty-eight post-Beatles studio albums and several bonus postscripts.

WINGS OVER AFRICA

In August 1973, Paul McCartney flew to Lagos, Nigeria, to record his fifth solo album. His entourage included bandmate/wife Linda, their two young daughters, rhythm guitarist Denny Laine and audio engineer Geoff Emerick.

Disaster struck just before the trip began. After weeks of rehearsals at McCartney's Scotland farm, the band's lead guitarist Henry McCullough and drummer Denny Seiwell quit over personal rifts and money scrapes. Touring act Wings was now a trio.

McCartney decided to press on. He and Linda believed that making a record overseas would be an exotic, exciting experience. Although EMI had studios around the world, they choose its most obscure location during Africa's monsoon season. Despite the rain and sweltering heat they settled into a six-week recording schedule.

During an early vocal overdub, McCartney turned ashen and gasped for air. Linda thought Paul was having a heart attack and rushed him to a Lagos hospital. They diagnosed a severe bronchial spasm, but somehow he returned to the recording studio the next day.

Early in 1973, actor Dustin Hoffman said he witnessed McCartney's on-the-spot songwriting process. Hoffman recalled meeting Paul in Jamaica while filming the movie *Papillon*. At a dinner party they exchanged stories about Pablo Picasso, who had recently died. McCartney picked up an acoustic guitar and spontaneously began to write a song about the famed artist's life. Hoffman said lyrics and melody flowed freely from McCartney. "Picasso's Last Words" would appear on the 1973 Lagos album.

Robbery

One steamy evening Paul and Linda decided to walk into the town of Apapa near EMI's studio. They were assaulted at knifepoint. Linda pleaded that the thieves not harm them. Instead they took Paul's camera, watch, wallet and rucksack. Inside the bag were all the new album's demo tapes and a notebook containing the song's lyrics and chord changes. While most rock stars would have booked the next plane home, the robbery didn't alter McCartney's course.

The Beatles early songs were written in hotel rooms and on tour buses. They were remembered by heart without the benefit of a tape recorder. Lennon and McCartney reasoned that if they couldn't memorize their material, why would their fans bother? Luckily, McCartney recalled most of the melodies and progressions. His Lagos song "Mrs. Vandebilt" references the robbery.

In 2015 I interviewed Wings guitarist Denny Laine about recording the Lagos album. "After the tapes were stolen, that was the end of those arrangements. Paul wrote most of the songs before we left for Africa. So we went back in and started over again. It was like a home studio, but we seemed to get a great feel. Paul played drums, I played guitar and we put the album together that way."

Wings guitarist Denny Laine at Fan Fest 2014

Another night a confrontation occurred at a local Nigerian nightspot. McCartney was berated by Afrobeat originator Fela Ransome-Kuti. The Lagos pop star accused McCartney of stealing Africa's music and beats. Kuti's aggressive behavior didn't stop until he heard the album's tracks at EMI's studio. In his 2006 memoir *Here, There and Everywhere*, Emerick said he showed Kuti that McCartney's new songs had few African influences or ethnic rhythms.

The Album

None of the trip's mishaps kept McCartney from creating one of rock's most compelling records. Nigeria's challenging conditions had steeled his musical vision. After adding backing vocals and orchestrations in London, McCartney released *Band on the Run* on December 5, 1973. Its nine songs included the famous title track plus "Jet," "Bluebird," "Mrs. Vandebilt," "Let Me Roll It," "Mamunia," "No Words," "Picasso's Last Words" and "Nineteen-Hundred and Eighty-Five." The up-tempo rocker "Helen Wheels" was included on the album's USA release.

Lennon and McCartney often crafted medleys and multi-part songs on the Beatles later albums. Many of *Band on the Run*'s songs are similarly interwoven. Its title track has three separate sections and both "Bluebird" and "Mamunia" have distinct tempo changes. Recording engineer Geoff Emerick said he highlighted McCartney's inventive bass playing on the record's final mix. Listen for his creative use of slurred triplets on "Mamunia's" descending baselines.

McCartney plays drums on each of the album's tracks, and his lead riff defines the song "Let Me Roll It." The album also features Linda McCartney's keyboard agility and her artistic use of the Moog synthesizer. Guitarist Laine received co-songwriting credit for "No Words," which combined two of his originals into one song.

The album spent two-and-a-half years on the pop record charts in the UK and USA. Four of its songs became hit singles. *Band on the Run* reached No.1 in America and was the UK's bestselling album in 1974. It also won Grammy Awards for Best Pop Performance of a Duo/ Group and Best Engineered Album.

Band on the Run wasn't conceived as a concept album, but its songs have a connected, cohesive feel. The tracks' stacked harmonies and tight arrangements remind one of the brisk vitality of *A Hard Day's Night*'s songs. Engineer Emerick said *Band on the Run* was "McCartney's shining moment as a solo artist." Take another listen; you might agree.

Capitol Records sleeve for single
Strawberry Fields Forever/Penny Lane.

TOPPERMOST OF THE
POPPERMOST: ALMOST

The Beatles reign on the British pop charts seemed almost
invincible. By 1967 they had tallied eleven No.1 Hit singles. Their

astounding run started in 1963 with 45 rpm "From Me to You" w/B-side "Thank You Girl" and continued with August 1966's release of "Yellow Submarine" w/double A-side "Eleanor Rigby." Then the Beatles dropped a bomb shell. The band's concert at San Francisco's Candlestick Park would be their final live show. The Beatles would no longer tour or perform in-concert, but instead focus solely on recording. Their decision was shocking and unprecedented. It stunned the rock world. During the previous six years the Beatles had played thousands of shows throughout Great Britain and in fourteen foreign countries. Wasn't it part of a rock band's DNA to play live shows?

The Beatles released their 7th studio LP *Revolver* before departing for the USA, but wouldn't perform a single cut from the new album on their final tour. Their new recordings were nearly impossible to play live over the tour's baseball stadium public address systems, which were drowned out by screaming fans. The Beatles were charting a new course, but London's Daily Mail and Telegraph Reporter speculated the band's decision was a precursor to their "split up."

After two months of recording at EMI's Abbey Road studios, manager Brian Epstein nervously urged producer George Martin to release a new Beatles single. On February 13, 1967 Parlophone/EMI rushed out "Penny Lane" and "Strawberry Fields Forever." Originally slated for the Beatles forthcoming album, the two remarkable, double-A sided

Lennon & McCartney songs seemed sure to be their twelfth No.1 UK single record.

A New Voice

After winning talent contests and singing in Leicester, England's working men's clubs, 20-year-old George Dorsey felt confident about moving to London to pursue his dream career. It was soon clear that the only vocal work Dorsey could find was singing in strip clubs. In 1958, he got his first showbiz break. He was hired to sing for 42 weeks on UK television show "Song Parade with the Grenadiers." Each week he performed whichever songs were topping the British charts. Dorsey thought he might be on the verge of finally making it as a singer. Guest appearances on British TV show "Oh Boy" and touring with pop singer Adam Faith buoyed his hopes. However Dorsey's fame was fleeting and his first recordings at Decca Records were flops. Then, in 1961, he came down with tuberculosis, which required a full year of recovery. Both his new car and the modest home he purchased for his parents were repossessed. Dorsey's short interlude with success felt like a cruel tease.

Two Masterpieces

John Lennon's opus "Strawberry Fields Forever" was composed during the fall of 1966 in Almeria, Spain, where he was acting in the movie "How I Won The War." Lennon's demos led to three recorded versions of the song and the two selected tracks were recorded in separate key signatures. Producer George Martin's technical skills brought the song's final mix into the same key. The composition took 45 hours to record with sessions stretched over five weeks. Lennon's vocals on "Strawberry Fields Forever" were double tracked and recorded at higher speed which produced a diffused, fluid effect. Contemporary recording artists often use a 'click track' to lay down a perfectly timed rhythm track to build upon. That technology didn't exist in the 1960s and is one of the reasons the Beatles music feels live and reaches out to listeners.

Sir Paul McCartney's "Penny Lane" opens a lyrical window to his Liverpool memories. Recorded in late December 1966 into mid-January 1967, the song features a penetrating piccolo trumpet solo played by Dave Mason of the Royal Philharmonic Orchestra. It was the first time the clear, high pitched trumpet sound was used in pop music. The history of "Penny Lane's" publishing/royalty rights followed a tangled path.

Before Australian businessman, Robert Holmes à Court sold the Northern Songs catalogue to Michael Jackson, he offered his daughter the rights to one Beatles song. He recommended she choose "Yesterday" given its royalty producing revenue. She turned him down flat and chose her favorite song "Penny Lane." To this day, Catherine Holmes à Court-Mather remains the sole copyright owner of McCartney's autobiographical musical ode.

Changing Names

Following the Beatles storyline, British singer Jerry Dorsey finally found someone who believed in him. Manager Gordon Mills felt that show business success began with the right image and name. Mills changed singer Thomas Woodward's name to Tom Jones, after seeing the 1963 British movie with the same name. He then helped the Wales vocalist score a 1965 No.1 UK Hit with "It's Not Unusual."

Mills felt Jerry Dorsey's name didn't have a show biz ring but he said found one that disc jockeys would find interesting. Mills nicked Dorsey's new name from a deceased 19th century German composer who wrote the music to opera Hansel & Gretel. He told Dorsey that his new stage name would be Engelbert Humperdinck. "It's a great name and it was so unusual. The name was so long that people thought it was a pop group," Humperdinck told Sue Lawley in a BBC radio interview.

His manager's next order of business was to find Humperdinck a new song to record. The tune he discovered was "Release Me (and Let Me Love Again)." It was written in 1949 by Eddie Miller and Robert Yount after the songwriters heard a couple arguing in a San Francisco bar. The unhappy wife pleaded to be released and set free from their marriage.

The song had been previously recorded by Patti Page, Ray Price and Kitty Wells and had done well on the USA country charts. Humperdinck's UK Decca Records version of "Release Me" was released on Jan. 12, 1967, but the 45rpm single was not an immediate hit. The song was rated "a miss" on British television show *Juke Box Joe*. The only jury member to score it "a hit" was British pop singer Lulu, whose '60s hits included "Shout" and "To Sir With Love."

In February 1967, Humperdinck received a last minute performance offer that changed his life and re-started his career. He was asked to replace pre-rock 'n' roll British vocalist, Dickie Valentine (who had fallen ill) on Britain's most popular television show "Sunday Night at the London Palladium." Humperdinck, who was now 30 yrs. old, sang "Release Me," which had been re-arranged by top UK music producer Charles Blackwell. The song had just eight lines of verse but Blackwell injected a dramatic key change into the mid-tempo ballad.

Humperdinck's emotive vocal and romantic presentation made it sing. "I took Dickie's place and just had 6 minutes to establish myself on the TV show stage. I went to rehearsal and I was shaking all over. It was the biggest show I ever did in my life and the greatest feeling I've ever had," Humperdinck remembered.

Chart Topper

After their long string of No.1 British Hits, the Beatles double A-sided single, "Penny Lane" w/ "Strawberry Fields Forever" would only reach No.2 on the UK charts. The day after Humperdinck's television performance, copies of "Release Me" flew off the record store shelves. His recording became the No.

Engelbert Humperdinck in concert 2018

1 UK single for six weeks in March/April 1967 and sold over 1.3 million copies. "Release Me" stayed on the charts for 56 consecutive weeks and was a chart topper in nine foreign countries.

In his autobiography "Engelbert: What's In A Name?" Humperdinck described the record's impact. "Penny Lane had great lyrics, you could visualize them. Their song had fabulous storytelling but it was so exciting for a person who had been living with holes in his shoes, having my first big record block the Beatles single from going to the top," he said. Humperdinck credits the Beatles for influencing his personal look and style. "I learned something from watching them perform. They all had the same hair style. When the Beatles sang that high "Woo" they shook their hair. Everything starts from the head," he said. "I had prematurely gray hair so I dyed my hair black and had wide sideburns. I grew them before Elvis and over the protests of my agent. I felt they were part of my image and then in the late 60's everybody started wearing them."

Engelbert soon became one of Las Vegas' top entertainers and at the height of his popularity he toured with 28 trunks of clothes including 150 shirts and both a personal dresser and hair stylist. Humperdinck also collected 14 rare Rolls Royce automobiles and once owned movie star Jayne Mansfield's Pink Place mansion on LA's Sunset Boulevard. He now maintains residences in both Los Angeles and his hometown Leicester, England.

Engelbert Humperdinck's 2018 show
at the Chumash Casino

Aftermath

Engelbert Humperdinck ruled the British single charts in the Spring of 1967, but the Beatles struck gold that same year in America. On March 18, 1967 "Penny Lane/Strawberry Fields Forever" reached the top of the USA Hot 100 Billboard chart. It was their eleventh No. 1 USA single record. Two months later "Release Me" climbed the same Billboard chart but only reached the #4 spot.

Humperdinck continues to play 90 concerts around the world each year and in February 2018 he performed at the Chumash Casino in Santa Ynez, California. Backed by a talented eight piece band, including two standout female singers, he sang his long string of hits including "The Last Waltz," "After The Lovin," "Welcome To My World," "A Man Without Love," "There Goes My Everything," "Spanish Eyes" and his anthem "Release Me."

Humperdinck knows how to deliver a song but he credits his mother's vocal genes. "She had an incredible operatic style voice and I think that's where I got my power from." He changes keys flawlessly and still has great stage presence. The "King of Romance" has sold 130 million records and continues to reign as an entertainer with a capital E. At the end of his interview, the now 82-year-old vocalist was asked how long he will continue perform? "There's no hang up time," Humperdinck said. "As long as I have my vocal powers and as long as the people out there want me, I'll be there for them."

MERSEYBEAT MUSIC QUIZ

The band's lexicon holds a treasure chest of Beatlesque trivia. Few may know Jack Lawrence wrote the 1942 popular song "Linda" about one-year old Linda Eastman. Twenty-seven years later she became the first wife of Paul McCartney. Did you know that London clothier Dougie Millings created more than 500 suits for the Beatles, including their famous collarless jackets? Here are a handful of Q&As to add to your Beatles repertoire.

One:

Q: How did drummer Richard Starkey Jr. become Ringo Starr?

A: Starkey changed his name to Ringo Starr well before he joined The Beatles. As the drummer for Rory Storm and the Hurricanes, Starkey usually wore two rings, which wasn't considered unusual.

According to Beatles biographer Mark Lewisohn, the first ring was a present from his mom when he turned sixteen. The second was an engagement ring given to him by his girlfriend Geraldine McGovern. Adding a third ring triggered his famous nickname. After his grandfather died, Starkey put on his granddad's gold wedding band, saying he would never remove it. Friends still called him "Richey" but in public he was soon known as "Rings."

Some speculate that Starkey's interest in country music and western movies prompted his name change. He had posters of Gene Autry, The Singing Cowboy, tacked to his teenage room walls. Others say Starkey borrowed the nickname Ringo from Johnny Ringo, the famed gunfighter at the OK Corral, or perhaps The Ringo Kid, who starred in the 1939 movie, *Stagecoach*. To complete his stage name transformation, Starkey clipped his last name in half and stenciled "Ringo Starr" on the Hurricane's bass drum.

In December 2015, Ringo sold at auction the pinky ring he wore on-stage with Rory Storm and at virtually every live Beatles show. Set in gold, the large synthetic blue "sapphire" fetched $106,250 at Julian's Auction in Beverly Hills, CA. Proceeds benefited Starr's Lotus Foundation.

Two:

Q: Did the Beatles release any instrumental songs?

A: The band's Parlophone albums contain one instrumental, "Flying," released on *Magical Mystery Tour*. "Flying" does contain several bars of background vocal "Ahhs." They also released three post-Beatles instrumentals: "Cayenne" (recorded in 1960), "Cry for a Shadow" (recorded in 1961) and "12 Bar Original" (recorded in 1965). All can be heard on their first two Anthology CDs.

Three:

Q: Which Beatles single 45 rpm record sold the most copies in England and the USA?

A: Released in 1963, Lennon and McCartney's single "She Loves You" sold over a million copies in the UK. The top American Beatles single hit was "Hey Jude," which sold eight million copies worldwide. Paul McCartney's 1977 solo recording of "Mull of Kintyre" sold two million copies in Great Britain but only climbed to No. 45 on the American (Easy Listening) Billboard chart.

Four:

Q: Which Beatles song was filmed for *A Hard Day's Night*, but didn't make the movie's final print?

A: John Lennon's "You Can't Do That" was filmed but later cut from the famous B/W film. Director Richard Lester decided there were too many songs in the London theater sequence, which re-creates a live Beatles show. Lennon sings lead and plays the guitar solo in "You Can't Do That." It was the first Beatles song to feature George Harrison's Rickenbacker electric twelve-string. You can see the cut performance on musician Phil Collins' documentary, which accompanies the 2014 remastered DVD of *A Hard Day's Night*. The Genesis drummer/vocalist (then a teenager) had a cameo role in the movie's theater scene.

Five:

Q: Which folk/pop artist influenced George Harrison's song "Something"?

A: James Taylor's first album contains the song "Something in the Way She Moves." The lyric is also the opening line to George Harrison's classic track "Something." Taylor's debut album was released on Apple Records in December 1968 with both McCartney and Harrison as guest performers. Harrison's song "Something" was finished in August 1969 and appeared on the *Abbey Road* album. In her memoir "Wonderful Tonight," Harrison's first wife, Pattie Boyd, states that he wrote the song about her.

Pattie Boyd 2016

Six:

Q: What do pop singer Tom Jones and drummer Ringo Starr share in common?

A: Both had life-threatening childhood illnesses. Ringo Starr was stricken twice. He developed appendicitis when he was six years old and fell into a three-day coma after surgery. He spent a year recovering in a Liverpool children's hospital. When both Ringo and Tom Jones were twelve, they independently contracted tuberculosis. Starr spent two years in a recovery program, and Jones was confined to bed for a year. He was not allowed to leave his Wales home for a second year.

Seven:

Q: What was British pop vocalist Cilla Black's real name?

A: Many popular singers adopt stage names. British vocalist Cliff Richard's birth name was Harry Rodger Web. Queen's lead singer Freddy Mercury was born as Frarroka Bulasra in Zanzibar off the East African coast. Cilla Black got her stage name by accident.

She was born in 1943 as Priscilla Marie Veronica White. Because her mother was also named Priscilla, she was called "Little Cilla." As a teenager she befriended the Beatles while working as a coat checker at Liverpool's Cavern Club. She occasionally made pop-up appearances as a vocalist with Rory Storm and the Hurricanes.

After she was discovered and signed by Beatles manager Brian Epstein, Liverpool's Merseybeat music magazine mistakenly printed her last name as Black rather than White. Epstein asked her to keep it as a stage name because of its dark, sexy image.

Black had one of early pop's purest voices. It was powerful, passionate and vulnerable. Apart from three appearances on the Ed Sullivan Show in the mid-'60s, she rarely performed in America. Her top UK Hits included "Anyone Who Had A Heart," "You're My World" and songs written by Lennon and McCartney. She also had her own BBC television variety show called *Cilla*. Her recording of "Alfie" (from the popular film) is sheer beauty. Find it on YouTube.com with composer Burt Bacharach conducting the live studio orchestra.

Eight:

Q: Who suggested that English vocalist Billy Kramer add the middle initial J. to his name?

A: Kramer's birth name was William Howard Ashton. After being signed by Brian Epstein in 1963, the pop singer randomly picked stage name Billy Kramer from a phone book. It was John Lennon who suggested Kramer add the initial J. to his name to give it flair.

He released the Lennon and McCartney ballad "Do You Want To Know A Secret" before it was featured on their *Please Please Me* album. Kramer's song "Bad To Me," written by John Lennon was a Top Ten Hit in America in 1964.

Nine, Number Nine, Number Nine...

Q: What compelled John Lennon to focus on the number nine in *White Album* song "Revolution 9?"

A: In a 1980 interview for David Sheff's book *All We Are Saying*, Lennon remarked, "I lived at 9 Newcastle Road (Liverpool) and I was born on the ninth of October. It's a number that follows me around." Other Lennon "nine" coincidences include the Beatles' first appearance at the Cavern Club on February 9, 1961, their February 9, 1964 debut on the Ed Sullivan Show and Yoko and John's son Sean being born on October 9, 1975.

Lennon said he assembled random tape loops to make the experimental sound montage that became "Revolution 9." One of the effects he used was the voice of an EMI announcer saying, 'This is EMI Test series number 9.' In his 1970 *Rolling Stone* interview Lennon remarked, "I just cut up whatever (the audio engineer picked) and I'd number nine it... It was like a joke bringing nine into it all the time. That's all it was."

Ten:

Q: Who inspired Paul McCartney's lyrics in his song "Band On The Run?"

A: McCartney said the initial spark for the album came from George Harrison during a 1970 Apple Records business meeting. As the Beatles imploded over management and contract problems, Harrison said he felt they were "all prisoners in some way." He wondered if they would "ever get out of here." McCartney remembered Harrison's words and inserted them into the title track's lyrics. He also used the prisoner metaphor for the album's cover shot. The photo features Paul and Linda McCartney, Denny Laine and friends caught in a searchlight, posing as escaping convicts.

Bonus Question:

Q: What was the first 1960s British rock song to become a No.1 USA Hit?

A: *Hint:* It wasn't a Beatles love song.

The first British No.1 Hit in the USA was "Telstar" by The Tornados. The rock instrumental topped the Billboard charts in 1962. The song featured a keyboard instrument called the Univox Clavoline which produced a wobbly vibrato effect. The Clavoline was a forerunner of the analog Moog synthesizer. In 1963, The Ventures released a memorable up-tempo cover of "Telstar." The Beatles first No.1 USA Hit record was 1964's "I Want To Hold Your Hand."

HERE, THERE & EVERYTHING BEATLES
(Music, Media, Tribute Bands, Festivals & Tours)

Starting or expanding a Beatles album or singles collection can follow several paths. If you want to purchase rare or highly graded Beatles LPs or singles expect to pay several hundred dollars or much more per disc. Collectible used records have grades for both the album and single's vinyl condition and record covers/sleeves. It's important to know if the album is a first pressing, a reissue or a foreign pressed album. A good resource for vinyl record grading is the current edition of the Goldmine Record Album Price Guide. It is available at www.amazon.com or www.barnesandnoble.com for about $27.00.

The following symbols and descriptions are used to designate a vinyl record's condition/value:

- **Mint (M):** Records in perfect condition that have never been played and are usually still sealed.
- **Near Mint (NM):** Near Mint is usually the highest grade used by record dealers/stores. Nearly perfect condition means there is no perceptible noise or any noticeable defect during playback. Covers should have very little wear and no tears. This standard also applies

to anything included with the album like lyric sheets, posters or album inserts. The standard also applies to 45 rpm records. An album or single record graded NM should be in pristine condition.

- **Very Good Plus (VG+):** There should only be superficial defects on the record's vinyl surface and its playback must be almost perfect. Wear signs could include almost undetectable scratches that have little effect on the overall sound. There may be very slight wear on album covers or 45 rpm sleeves or inserts.

- **Very Good (VG):** There may be light scratches on the album or 45rpm with some noise heard during softer musical sections. Album covers and 45 rpm sleeves may be marked with writing.

- **Good (G):** The album or single won't skip but will have significant surface noise. The 45's sleeve or album's cover or side seam may be split or show considerable wear or fading.

- **Fair (F)** and **Poor (P):** A Fair-graded record may have significant noise during playback and occasionally skip. The only reason to buy a poor-graded record is for an art project. This vinyl grade indicates the record may be warped and will likely skip very badly.

Rare or highly-graded Beatles LPs and singles are often listed online at collectible record sites including eBay and can be found at select used record shops or their websites, including Rockaway Records in Los Angeles, CA. If your motivation is to find lower-priced, original Beatles Parlophone or Capitol Records albums or singles in very good playable condition, a well stocked used record store can often help you.

Make sure you have researched the relative value of the Beatles album or single and determine whether the record you want to buy is an original or subsequent pressing. If the record is within your budget be sure to examine the condition of the LP's cover and vinyl surfaces under a strong light. Remember that used Beatles albums are over fifty years old and you can't expect to have an absolutely perfect copy unless you are willing to tap your savings account. Take your time to examine each single/album because it's a bummer to return home and find you've overlooked a serious flaw. The record shop should also offer to play the album/single during your inspection. Consider using headphones if you are buying an expensive record.

I recently bought four used Capitol Records Beatles albums (*Rubber Soul*, *Yesterday & Today*, *Yellow Submarine* and *Let It Be*) all in very good playable condition (VG+) with covers in decent condition (VG) for $65 plus tax at American Pie Records in Ventura, CA. I received a nice discount because I purchased all four records at the same time. The store had several copies of each album and all the LP's were subsequent pressings.

If you purchase new Beatles CDs or Vinyl on Amazon. com and subscribe to Amazon Prime you may be given digital access to each track you have purchased. Check carefully to see if the CD you want is 'Auto Rip' eligible. If that option is not available it's easy to rip your new Beatles CD to your computer using a built-in or remote CD burner and downloading it to your smart phone. You can listen to the album in Amazon Prime's offline mode through earphones or a Bluetooth speaker.

Paperback Writers

One of the exciting outcomes of publishing a music biography is meeting other Beatles authors. At the 2017 *Chicago Fest For Beatles Fans* I was introduced to Robert Rodriquez, whose book *Revolver* details how the Beatles seventh studio album re-imagined rock 'n' roll. Sitting to my left was Jerry Hammack, a Canadian recording engineer whose books, The *Beatles Recording Reference Manuals*, document the equipment and instruments used in every Beatles EMI recording session. To my right was Kit O'Toole who writes for Beatlefan Magazine and is the author of *Songs We Were Singing*. Her book takes readers on a stroll through rarely discussed Beatles tracks.

Perched nearby was author Ken Womack who has published two great biographies of the life of producer George Martin, titled *Maximum Volume* and *Sound Pictures*. Deciding which Beatles books to add to your library depends on your focus. Getting an autographed Beatles edition is a fun outcome of attending a Beatles festival or book signing and authors are happy to answer any Beatles related questions you may have.

Collecting Beatles biographies from source authors is a great way to start or expand your collection. The Beatles weighty *Anthology* autobiography, published in 2000 and Hunter Davis' authorized 1965 biography of the band, may be the most important source Beatles books. Hopefully Apple Publishing will decide to resize the Beatles *Anthology* and make it easier to enjoy.

Reading John Lennon's books, (*In His Own Write* and *A Spaniard in the Works*) give fans insight to his vivid lyrical imagination. My

1981 compilation of both works features Paul McCartney's smart introduction. In 1995 Yoko Ono published *Skywriting by Word of Mouth*, prose written by her husband when they lived in New York City. Ms. Ono's 1964 book of poetry entitled, *Grapefruit* was a preface to the couple's subsequent musical partnership.

There are over one thousand Beatles books and biographies listed on Amazon.com. It seems that almost everyone associated with the band has written about their personal experiences. On the recording side, Beatles producer George Martin and Sgt. Pepper engineer Geoff Emrick's biographies are important firsthand recording studio primers. Two of the most compelling personal memoirs were penned by Beatles wives Cynthia Lennon and Patti Boyd. Neither Paul McCartney's former fiancée Jane Asher or Yoko Ono have chosen to share their written memories. Apple Records executive/Beatles road manager Neil Aspinall consciously decided not to write an autobiography before he died in 2008 and personal assistant Mal Evans was tragically shot and killed by the Los Angeles Police Department in 1976 before his personal diaries could be published.

Mark Lewisohn is often cited as the Beatles most recognized historian. His books are highly recommended and include *The Complete Beatles Recording Sessions*, *The Beatles in London* and *Tune In, the Beatles: All These Years*. Other noted Beatles writers include prolific scribe Bruce Spizer and Liverpool author David Bedford, whose new book documents the twenty-three drummers who played with the Beatles.

Contemporary
Vedic Library Series

CHANT
AND BE HAPPY
The Power of Mantra Meditation

BASED ON THE TEACHINGS OF HIS DIVINE GRACE
A.C. BHAKTIVEDANTA SWAMI PRABHUPĀDA
Founder-*Ācārya* of the International Society for Krishna Consciousness

Featuring Exclusive Conversations with

JOHN LENNON and GEORGE HARRISON

172

Dhani Harrison's Pop-up Show

One of the most unusual Beatles books was given to me in 2009 at Dhani Harrison's (George's son) pop-up concert in Isla Vista, CA located next to the University of California, Santa Barbara. Harrison's band (*thenew#2*) performed for free on an elevated stage with a professional sound system in a local park. After his hour long set Dhani came to the stage barrier to greet fans under the watch of his bodyguards. Standing next to me were two Hare Krishna women dressed in bright orange robes who were overjoyed to talk with Dhani and said they had traveled from a Washington DC temple to attend his "unannounced" concert. As we parted, the Krishna women gave me a paperback book, *Chant and Be Happy*, which features George Harrison's and John Lennon's photos on its cover and a long interview with George conducted in 1982 by Hare Krishna elder Mukunda Goswami.

Rock Magazines

Rolling Stone Magazine was my go-to source for Beatles reporting until the rock landscape changed. After straying into investigative journalism and pop culture it looks like Rolling Stone is back covering contemporary and classic rock and featuring legendary writers like Rob Sheffield and David Fricke.

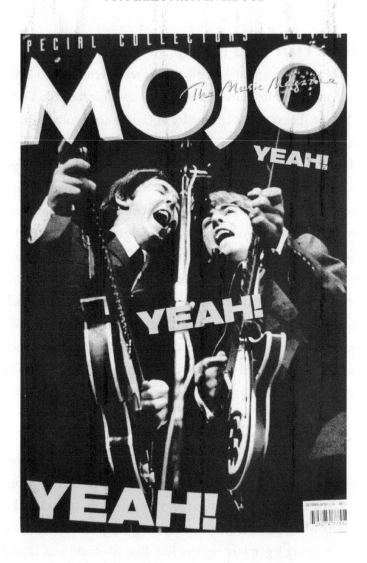

Mojo Magazine (published in England) continues to feature regular coverage of the Beatles. What's great about Mojo is that the cover price ($11.99 US) also includes a free CD.

(www.mojomagazine.com). A past *Mojo* CD featured fifteen 1950's songs that powered the Beatles, from "A Taste of Honey," sung by Billy Dee Williams to the Top Notes original version of "Twist and Shout." The same issue also included a deep look at Ron Howard's Beatles documentary, *Eight Days A Week: The Touring Years.* There were also two bonus color posters of the Beatles 1963 London Palladium and the handbill for their 1966 Candlestick Park concert. Other recent issues included an extended interview with Paul McCartney about 2018's *Egypt Station* album and a CD of contemporary Liverpool bands.

Mojo Publications special issues include their 2017-18 Beatles collector series, priced at $16.00 US. *The Red Issue* covers the Beatles from 1962-1966 (leaving Liverpool to George Harrison's first visit to India) with articles penned by Barry Miles and Mark Lewisohn. *The Blue Issue* covers events of 1967–1970 (the Magical Mystery Tour, Rishikesh, John & Yoko highlights) and is framed with rare Beatles photos, great graphics and standout prose. Both can be purchased online.

The music collectors monthly, *Goldmine Magazine's* articles have included the backstory of how "I Want To Hold Your Hand" jumped from chart position #35 to No.1 in just one week and insider coverage of "Yellow Submarine's" 50th Anniversary re-release. Another music newspaper worth reading is *Record Collector News* published seven times a year and is available free at used record shops on the West Coast, Chicago and New York City. US/International subscriptions are available at: www.recordcollector.com.

The British Beatles Fan Club Magazine is printed on glossy paper and published quarterly in England. It's a treat to receive a Beatles magazine from London every three months. Each issue includes an updated calendar of worldwide Beatles events, fan letters in a Q&A format and a funny feature entitled the Crap Photo which spotlights the issue's worst Beatles photographic effort. (www.britishbeatlesfanclub.com).

Beatlefan Magazine (www.beatlefanmagazine.com) is headquartered in Atlanta, Georgia and published six times a year in newsprint with glossy front and back covers. Because of its larger format, Beatlefan offers longer, in-depth articles and subscribers are treated to the magazine's Beatles News Roundup and features including Hard Day's Net which focuses on what's happening online in Beatleworld.

Movies & Videos

In 2012, I attended Scott Freiman's *Deconstructing The Beatles* multi-media presentation in Los Angeles and was so impressed that three months later I flew to Denver to see him deconstruct the Beatles Sgt. Pepper and Rubber Soul albums. If you can't attend one of Freiman's shows in-person, his presentations can now be streamed online or purchased as DVDs. (www.scottfreiman.com).

The four essential Beatles movies every fan should own include the 4k digital restoration (approved by Director Richard Lester) of 1964's *A Hard Day's Night*, the digitally restored 1965 film *"Help"* which includes an enhanced soundtrack, fifty-two minute long *"Magical Mystery Tour"* released in 1967 and the animated film *"Yellow Submarine,"* which includes a delightful cameo of the band at the movie's end. "Yellow Submarine" was first released in 1968 but in 2018 it was re-released for a short theatrical run with enhanced graphics and a crystalline soundtrack. All four films can be purchased online for about $100.

I was given a bootleg copy of Beatles 1970 documentary *Let It Be*, but the film has not been commercially available since the 1980s. Its highlights include Lennon and Ono joyfully waltzing to George Harrison's song "I, Me, Mine" and the complete Beatles 1969 London rooftop concert. Martin Scorsee's 2011 documentary of George Harrison, *Living in the Material World*, paints a brilliant portrait of the band's lead guitarist with archrival footage, home movies and backstage interviews. The 2013 film, *Good Ol' Freda* remembers Beatlemania through the lens and stories of Beatles Fan Club Secretary Freda Kelly. I was fortunate to meet Ms. Kelly at the 2014 *Los Angeles Fest for Beatles Fans* and was struck by her friendly, unassuming manner.

Another documentary film to consider is Warner Brother's 2005 release, *Imagine: John Lennon*, which combined Lennon's personal film archives with its thirty-six song soundtrack. The film was re-cut by Yoko Ono in 2018 adding fifteen additional minutes of John Lennon's live studio performance with Klaus Voormann playing bass guitar. Documentary filmmaker Seth Swirsky traveled across the USA interviewing dozens of top musicians, studio legends and rock personalities about their encounters and relationships with The Beatles. His terrific film *Beatles Stories* includes interviews with Badfinger's lead guitarist Joey Molland, Door's keyboardist Ray Manzarek, Sir George Martin, rock photographer Henry Diltz, Peter Noone, May Pang, Donovan, Klaus Voormann, Davey Jones, and Art Garfunkel who is interviewed on his balcony high above New York's Central Park.

The major motion picture, *I Want To Hold Your Hand*, hit theaters in 1978. The film follows the antics of six New Jersey teens intent on meeting the Beatles in New York City in 1964. It's a fun romp worth seeing primarily because it was co-written and directed by Robert Zemeckis. The *Everly Brothers Reunion Concert* filmed in 1983 at Royal Albert Hall shows why the 50's singing duo was the Beatles harmonic template. It is one of the best live concert films ever released.

Fab Four's Founder Ron McNeil

To tribute artists, the word "imitation" means paying homage. The Fab Four are one of the USA's most successful Beatles tribute acts. They've had residencies in Las Vegas and have toured South America, Europe and Asia. In 2013, the group received an Emmy Award for its PBS TV Special. I caught up with Fab Four founder Ron McNeil during a recent concert tour.

Q: How did the Fab Four come together?

Ron McNeil: I formed the group in 1997 after going to a Beatles convention. I saw Ardy Sarraf performing with his group there. He was singing a song by McCartney called "Coming Up" and the hair on the back of my neck literally stood up. I said to myself, 'I've found my tribute band member to play Paul McCartney.' His act won the sound-alike contest that year. The next year I won the solo singing competition performing John Lennon's song "Imagine."

Q: After almost twenty years playing Beatles music, what have you learned about their creative process?

McNeil: At first you're in awe of it all. Then you learn some of the music's intricacies. I always go to their records to find out who's doing what. I ask, why does this sound so good? Lennon mainly carried the melody. George would be somewhere in-between John and Paul. McCartney had the higher top parts. When both of them were singing together it had that Everly Brothers sound — singing in thirds. It wasn't so much what notes they were singing but how and when they were singing harmony that was crucial. The Beatles instincts were very good there.

Q: How does The Fab Four fit into the Beatles legacy?

McNeil: I think we've been brought into their hurricane. What we add to the legacy is putting their music on stage and performing it. We're the only 'four-piece' Beatles tribute that plays everything live. Other groups play to a backing track or have vocals on tape. It is hard to do everything live, and sometimes you don't have enough fingers to carry all the parts. We arrange them for a four-man band and still make them sound true to their records. People overlook that one of the reasons the Beatles were so successful is that their songs are about peace and love. Emotions that people relate to. For the most part, their music was about things people cherish.

Q: Has their music affected you personally?

McNeil: We're Beatles fans first. We happen to be performing their music but if we were sitting in the audience I'd still be enjoying it. There are Beatles tracks that touch everyone in certain ways. I hope The Fab Four's show stirs up some of those memories.

Q: Has the band ever performed in Liverpool?

Ron McNeil (far rt.) with Fab Four 2013

McNeil: Oh yeah, we played at the Cavern Club. It was like going to the holy land for a Beatles fan. The minute you land you get a feeling of who they really were. It gives you another perspective on their legacy. It's different from the picture you have of four moptop guys with skinny ties. It's amazing that the best songwriters, right up there with Mozart and Beethoven, came out of Liverpool.

Beatles Tribute Acts

In addition to The Fab Four, here are the best Beatles acts I've heard over the last decade:

- Tribute act *Rain* includes a mind blowing multi-media show while they roll through songs from each of the Beatles albums. They are a major touring act and must-see artists.
- *The Fab Faux* musical tribute includes Will Lee, former bassist for the David Letterman Show and Jimmy Vivino, former guitarist of TV host the Conan O'Brian's house band. They perform the Beatles repertoire note for note and feature songs the Beatles never played live. They're often accompanied by additional musicians referred to as the Hogshead Horns and the Cream Tangerine Strings. Highly recommended act.

- *Liverpool* has been the *Fest for Beatles Fans* house band since the late 1970s. Led by superb bassist/vocalist Glen Burtnik, Liverpool played a brilliant rendition of George Harrison's "Within You, Without You" at the 2017 Chicago Fest For Beatles Fans. They have supported Fest guests including Harry Nilsson, Billy Preston and Donovan. Both Burtnik and lead guitarist John Merjave also are in New Jersey Beatles act, The Weeklings who also perform an original repertoire. Their impressive 2018 concert is reviewed in the 2018 White Album Symposium chapter.
- Los Angeles area Beatles act *The Baja Bugs* feature a wild, charismatic drummer with real snap and top singing chops. They're regulars at the San Diego Beatles Fair.
- *Sgt. Pepper* of Ventura, California features outstanding guitarists who play stunning dual leads on songs like "This Bird Can Sing." This act may be the most reasonably priced, highly-rated Beatles tribute band on the West Coast.
- Regional touring act *Abbey Road* performs material from each Beatles era in regional circuit clubs and at larger venues. Their multiple costume changes are part of the evening's fun.
- *The Mersey Beatles* are a must see in Liverpool at The Cavern Club or on their next USA tour. They've been together since 1999 and still perform like there's no tomorrow.

Radio Shows

The Beatles official satellite radio station is found on Sirius XM's Channel 18 and features the band's catalogue of hits, selected rarities, solo works and a schedule that includes both Chris Carter's *Breakfast with The Beatles* show and Peter Asher's program *From Me To You*. Sirius XM offerings also include *The Fab Forum* call-in show curated by Dennis Elsas, Bill Flanagan with special guests like Tom Frangione. Sir Paul McCartney and Sir Ringo Starr were enthusiastic supporters of the new channel and the response by listeners has been positive. Sirius XM service can cost $11-$22 per month depending on the package you select (www.sirusxm.com) but various discounts are usually available by shopping online and/or paying in advance for a year of service.

There are a variety of hosted Beatles radio programs across the USA including Dennis Mitchell's *Breakfast with The Beatles* show which is broadcast live on Santa Barbara, CA's classic rock station KTYD-FM. It's also syndicated each week on 60 radio stations across the USA and in Germany, Sweden, New Zealand and is heard in London and Liverpool. Britain's longest running Beatles themed radio program is *Pete Dick*'s show which is heard on Tamworth FM in England and can be found on The Wall internet radio station.

Blogs & Podcasts

Almost every major Beatles rock writer has a blog site and often magazines like *Beatlefan* and *The British Beatles Fan Club* offer extra value to their subscribers with updated internet blogs. Beatles blogs are often fairly short, casual conversations with readers rather than long, one-off articles. Don't pay for a blog, vlog or podcast as there are dozens to sample for free. With Facebook's added video features, podcasters can now conduct live video chats with several guest presenters on the same screen and both receive and respond to viewer questions in real time. One of the Beatles writers embracing this new technology is Chicago Facebook video-caster Kit O'Toole. She's the co-host of *Talk More Talk* featuring Beatles experts including author Ken Womack, Tom Hunyady (also co-host of *2Legs: A Paul McCartney Podcast*) and Ken Michaels (co-host of syndicated radio show *Things We Said Today* on the air for 36 years). Another internet podcast to check out is author Robert Rodriquez's *Something About The Beatles* show. Don't forget to listen to Lanea Stagg's and Jude Southerland Kessler's radio podcast "*She Said, She Said.*" Their 2018–19 series includes a five episode debate on the Beatles vs. Stones.

Beatles Festivals

Attending a Beatles Festival can feel like musical pilgrimage. Fans often travel across the country and around the world to attend annual Fests and renew friendships formed in the Beatles community. It's amazing to listen to "amateur" musicians who gather in the festival's hotel lobbies and perform Beatles songs late into the night. Festivals usually feature a large marketplace with Beatles gear and memorabilia, book signings and include top musical artists and great Beatles tribute acts. Here's a listing of the most well known Beatles Festivals across the USA and England.

- The annual *Fest for Beatles Fans* is held at a major hotel located in the New York Metro area each March and in Chicago every August. See www.thefest.com for the fest's dates/location, musical line-up, reserved tickets and hotel and airplane discounts. *The Fest for Beatles Fans* is the longest running Beatles event in the USA and Fest Director Mark Lapidos and his family work hard to make each year's event memorable. They consistently bring together the country's top musicians, Beatles authors and special guests including former members of McCartney's band Wings, John Lennon's sister Julia Baird, Billy J. Kramer, Peter Asher and many, many others.
- The *San Diego Beatles Fair* takes place at Queen Bee's Arts and Cultural Center in the North Park section of San Diego, CA. The two day event features one major Beatles related act and non-stop music from a dozen tributes bands and solo artists. I've been to this two-day festival twice and recommend it especially to those who live on the West Coast. See: www.sandiegobeatlesfair.com.

- *Beatles at The Ridge Festival* is held annually (in September) in Walnut Ridge, Arkansas. This three-day fest features a dozen Beatles acts and an author's symposium. Past bands have included the *Liverpool Legends* whose members were hand-picked by George Harrison's sister Louise. See: www.beatlesattheridge.com

- The *New Orleans Beatles Festival* is presented each July by the William Credo Agency at the House of Blues club located at 225 Decatur St. in the city's famed French Quarter. New Orleans area acts and bands perform Beatles sets all weekend. www.williamcredoagency.com.

- The *Abbey Road on the River* (Beatles Fest) occurs each year over Memorial Day weekend in Jeffersonville, Indiana. The 2019 eclectic music event will feature The Buckinghams, The Grass Roots, The Cowsills, the Classicstone Band performing the entire Abbey Road album, the Magic Bus Band presenting music from 1969's Woodstock festival and a tribute saluting The Who's *Tommy* album. That's quite a line-up! Contact: www.arotr.com.

- The *International Beatles Week* in Liverpool, England takes place each year during the last week in August. Over 70 bands, acoustic artists and jam acts from 20 countries perform, including Brazil where the Beatles remain wildly popular. In 2018, International Beatles week was paired down to a four day festival but the music goes on each night until 4am or 5am. Ticket packages with accommodations and special theater shows sell-out early each year. Contact: www.internationalbeatlesweek. com and make sure you plan your trip and get concert tickets and lodging six to eight months in advance.

BEATLES TOURS

London

Many of the highlights of my Beatles tours of London and Liverpool are described in my Postcards From England chapter of the book. In London, I took both of Richard Porter's Beatles Walks (www.beatlesinlondon.com) during my 2015 Beatles trip. The first began outside the Marylebone Underground Station, which was featured in the opening scenes of film *A Hard Day's Night*. After Mr. Porter collected the ten pound fee (8 pounds for seniors and/or full-time students) he showed our small group the exact locations depicted in the film. We strolled past the registry where Paul and Linda McCartney were married on our way to Ringo Starr's London flat. Across a small park was Paul McCartney's MPL Communications brick building where he oversees his many musical enterprises. Porter's second walk began outside the Tottenham Court Road Underground and spotlighted the studio where "Hey Jude" was recorded, the former Apple

Records headquarters on Savile Row and included a walk down colorful Carnaby Street.

All of Porter's London Beatles tours include an inexpensive, short subway ride to the St. John's Wood Tube Station (not included in the tour fee) which is three blocks from Abbey Road Studios and its famous crosswalk. It's remarkable that more tourists aren't injured while posing in the celebrated walkway. London's drivers are amazingly patient with Abbey Road's Beatles fans. Porter's walks don't require to you pre-book, rather just show-up at the designated time and tour location, pay your fee and off you go. He keeps a brisk pace, so wear comfortable shoes and stay near the guide to hear his constant commentary. There are certainly other London Beatles walking tours and private coach/van tours worth considering, but expect to pay several times the cost of this tour. Before traveling to London consider reading "The Beatles London," which chronicles everything Beatles in London and costs less than $20 on Amazon.com.

New York City Beatles Tour

I met Beatles expert Susan Ryan at the 2018 International White Album Symposium. She lives in Brooklyn and takes Beatles fans on individual and small group NYC tours (Fab Four NYC Walking Tours). She has a buoyant personality and knows how to navigate NYC's streets. Beatles tour sites include Lennon's Dakota Apartments, the Strawberry Fields Memorial in Central Park and press conference locations at the Plaza Hotel, where the Beatles stayed in 1964 while appearing on the Ed Sullivan Show. Susan Ryan's two hour tour costs $40 per person and $70 for individual tours. Contact: nycwalkingtours@gmail.com or call 917-414-3315.

Beatles Hamburg

Stafanie Hempel's Hamburg, Germany evening Beatles tour is endorsed by former Beatles Fan Club Secretary Freda Kelly. The 2 ½ to 3 hour tour is available every Saturday night, from April through November.

Contact: info@hemplemusik.de. The 28 Euro tour fee ($32 US) includes admission to Hamburg's St. Pauli Museum. The tour is conducted in German and English.

Los Angeles Beatles Tour

All four of the Beatles maintained homes in Los Angeles. "Blue Jay Way," located in the Hollywood Hills became the title of George Harrison's song on *The Magical Mystery Tour* album. Englishwoman Gillian Thomas guides fans to Los Angeles Beatles sites including the Bel-Air home where the band met Elvis, the Troubadour Club where John Lennon was ejected and the landmark Capitol Records building where all four Beatles Hollywood Stars are located. The 3.5 to 4 hour tour costs $75 per person. Contact: www.amagicalmystertour.com.

Beatles Liverpool

One of Liverpool's great private tour guides is Beatles author David Bedford at: www.davdbedford.com. The Liverpool native lives near Penny Lane and has penned books including *Liddypool*, *The Fab Four* and *Finding the Fourth Beatle*. He will take you to rare Beatles sites other tours may miss. If you don't mind a larger group experience jump on the *Magical Mystery Tour Bus* (cost: 19 pounds per ticket) which leaves several times each day from the Beatles Story Museum located at Albert Docks. Sit on the right side of the bus, near the front for the best view. You'll stop at the gates to Strawberry Fields, visit Paul McCartney's childhood home (from the outside), glide down Penny Lane and 2 hours later end up at the Cavern Club on Mathew Street. The free souvenir this tour promises is a postcard of the famous Cavern Club.

The Magical Mystery Tour Bus a great introduction to the Beatles Liverpool haunts, but I would also recommend pre-booking the National Trust Beatles docent led tours of both John Lennon's 'Mendips' and Paul McCartney's 20 Forthlin Road homes. The other tours don't take you inside either house. See: www.nationaltrust.org.uk for times/days that docent tours are offered. You can also email the National Trust at: thebeatleshomes@nationaltrus.org.uk. The tour costs 24 pounds for adults and 7 pounds for children. When you've finished your day of Beatles sightseeing, take time to walk, shop and eat in downtown Liverpool. I'd also recommend taking the Liverpool ferry across the River Mercy to Birkenhead and back. It's a memory you'll carry forever.

AUTHOR'S INTERVIEW

Author Mark Brickley
Penny Lane, Liverpool

Q: What were the most unexpected facets of your trip to Liverpool?

Mark Brickley: The friendliness of the city... The lush landscape where Lennon and McCartney grew up. It's so green and leafy... Harrison's and Starr's row homes were more modest... Finding that the Hard Day 's Night Hotel is located just around the corner from the Cavern Club on Mathew Street... Learning that "Scouse" (the descriptive name of Liverpool's droll accent) is also a tasty, spicy meat and potato stew... My lodgings in Liverpool cost less than $100 US per night.

Q: Where did you stay in London?

Brickley: I stayed at the Radisson Blu Edwardian Vanderbilt Hotel in London. My $280 per night single room was very small but included a fabulous English breakfast buffet and great coffee. It kept me fueled for hours. The hotel is located less than a block from the Gloucester Road Tube station and four blocks from Royal Albert Hall. I traveled to the hotel from Heathrow Airport using the Underground.

Q: Did you use the Tube while touring Beatles sites in London?

Brickley: Yes, it's often crowded but the Tube/Underground is the quickest way to get around London. I rode it to see the Beatles lyrics exhibit at the British Library and also to the departure points for my two London Beatles walking tours. The first trek began at the Marylebone Station which was featured in the opening scene of the Beatles movie *A Hard Day's Night*.

Q: How many countries did the Beatles perform in?

Brickley: From 1960 through their final 1966 international tour, the Beatles performed in fourteen countries outside the United Kingdom (England, Wales, Northern Ireland and Scotland). The Beatles played in Italy, Spain, Germany, Sweden, Denmark, Holland, France, USA, Canada, Japan, The Philippines, New Zealand, the territory of Hong Kong and Australia.

Beatles Wow Australia

On June 12, 1964 nearly 200,000 fans turned out to greet the Beatles when they arrived in Adelaide, Australia. It was the biggest crowd ever assembled to greet the band. Ringo Starr rejoined the tour in Melbourne after spending nearly two weeks in a London hospital with acute tonsillitis. Ringo's stand-in was British drummer Jimmie Nicol, who played in eight of the Beatles twenty Australian shows. Nichols received 5,000 letters from Australian fans and later inspired Paul McCartney to write the song "Getting Better," which appeared on the *Sgt. Pepper* album.

According to biographer Hunter Davis, McCartney said he asked the fill-in drummer how he was bearing up. Nicol drolly replied: "It's getting better…"

Q: What was your impression of the Beatles inspired Cirque du Soleil "Love" show in Las Vegas?

Brickley: I saw the updated Mirage Hotel Cirque du Soleil show in 2016. Cirque's "Love" performance transports the audience into a Beatles dream. The show's soundtrack includes dozens of Beatles songs with emphasis on the Sgt. Pepper era. One of the production's most pleasing Beatles medleys features "Good Night" from the *White Album* combined with *Abbey Road*'s "Octopus Garden." George and Giles Martin's orchestration seamlessly blend the songs together.

Paul McCartney, Ringo Starr, Yoko Ono, Sean Lennon, Olivia Harrison, Dhani Harrison and Giles Martin (son of George Martin) were all on hand to celebrate the "Love" show's tenth anniversary. The production streams vivid Beatles imagery on two 60′ × 25′ video screens that encircle the theater-in-the-round audience. Computerized projectors cast wild colors and patterns over the entire surface of the Love Theater stage.

The show features seventy performers including aerialists, acrobats, amazing skaters and trampoline artists. Some of "Love's" most charming stagecraft involves performers in minor roles. The show's narrator is a carnival barker with a quirky, engaging sense of humor. A spirited mime wanders by, trying to find a performer who will accept his bright yellow flowers. Another colorfully dressed actor pours puffy, dry-ice steam from a large silver teapot into audience members' cocktails.

Neon sculpture at the Mirage Hotel's Beatles "Love" Show

Tickets to the *Cirque du Soleil Beatles* show start at $59. My upgraded seat (section 205, row N) cost $94 including the $12 Ticketmaster fees. After the performance ended, the audience poured into the Beatles store located next door. The Mirage Hotel shop is the only licensed Apple Ltd. Beatles store in the USA.

On Tour: Las Vegas

The Beatles flew from San Francisco to Las Vegas on August 20, 1964. It was the second stop of their nationwide tour covering twenty-two US cities. The band's first movie, *A Hard Day's Night*, had been released a month earlier and Beatlemania was in full swing. Two thousand screaming fans met the band's chartered plane at 1:00 am. The Beatles stayed in a top floor suite at the Sahara Hotel and met flamboyant pianist Liberace backstage before their performance.

The Liverpool quartet performed two sold-out shows (4pm and 9pm) at the 7,500 seat Las Vegas Convention Hall with tickets ranging from $2.50 to $5.50. They received a minimum appearance fee of $25,000, against sixty-percent of the venue's gate receipts. Singer Jackie De Shannon was the opening act and the Beatles added cover "Till There Was You" to their standard twelve-song set list. The 1964 concerts were the only time that all four Beatles performed together in Las Vegas.

Q: What was your experience at John Lennon's memorial in NYC's Central Park?

Brickley: Lennon's "Strawberry Fields" is located in New York City just off Central Park West near 72nd St. It's directly across the street from The Dakota building where Lennon and his wife Yoko Ono lived. She still resides there.

I visited the Strawberry Fields memorial gardens on a crisp May afternoon in 2016. Thirty feet into Central Park, an artist was selling hand-painted Lennon postcards — I bought two. Twenty steps further there were a dozen visitors posing for photos around the square's tiled "Imagine" center piece. A musician was playing for tips and asked if I had a favorite song. I gave him my change and he played a powerful cover of Lennon's "In My Life." As a coda I yelled, "He's still with us!" to whoever was listening. It was a connecting point, an exclamation of empathy, respect and hope.

John Lennon's NYC "Strawberry Fields"

ABOUT THE AUTHOR

Music journalist Mark Brickley has published dozens of interviews, articles and music columns in the *Coastal View News, Ojai Quarterly Magazine, Deep Magazine, Carpinteria Magazine* and online at *Noozhawk.com*. Mark's photographs often accompany his columns and articles. He is also a performing musician and his music videos can be found on www.YouTube.com and his recordings "Berkeley Hills," "Lincoln's Lament" and "Love Finds Everyone" are available on iTunes and CD Baby. He lives near Santa Barbara, CA.

ACKNOWLEDGMENTS

Thanks to Sylvia Weller for her never-ending assistance and encouragement. I appreciate the insights and help from filmmaker Larry Nimmer of www.nimmer.net. Thanks to my copy editor, Esther Baruch of www.finishingtouchesediting. com and proof editing by Carpinteria editor Peter Durge and entertainment attorney/songwriter Ted Baer. I appreciate the skills of my website designer Garret Matsuura of www. arclightmedia.com. Thanks also to Anthony Puttee and his staff at the Self-Publishing Lab in Brisbane, Australia for the book's cover design and formatting.

BIBLIOGRAPHY

Beatles, The. *The Beatles Anthology*. San Francisco: Chronicle Books LLC, 2000.

Boyd, Pattie. *Wonderful Tonight*. New York: Three Rivers Press, 2007.

Brown, Peter. *The Love You Make*. New York: New American Library, 2002.

Coleman, Ray. *Lennon*. New York: McGraw-Hill, 1984.

Cooke de Herrera, *Nancy. Beyond Gurus*. Nevada City, CA: Blue Dolphin Publishing, 1993.

Cott, Jonathan. *Days I'll Remember*. New York: Knopf Doubleday Publishing Group, 2013.

Davis, Hunter. *The Beatles*. New York: W.W. Norton & Company, 1968 and 2009.

DiLello, Richard. *The Longest Cocktail Party*. Los Angeles: Alfred Music, 2014.

Emerick, Geoff. *Here, There and Everywhere*. New York: Gotham Books, 2007.

Goldberg, Philip. *American Veda*. New York: Harmony Books, 2010.

Harry, Bill. *Love Me Do*. McLean, Virginia: Miniver Press LLC.2012.

Howlett, Kevin. *Sgt. Peppers Box Set*. Apple Records, 2018.

Ingham, Chris. *The Rough Guide to The Beatles*. London: Penguin Group, 2009.

Johnny Gentle and Ian Forsyth. *JG and The Beatles*. Amazon Kindle Book, 2005.

Kane, Larry. *Ticket to Ride*. Philadelphia: Running Press Books, 2003.

Leigh, Spencer. *The Beatles in Hamburg. Chicago: Chicago Review Press, 2011.*

Lennon, Cynthia. *John*. New York: Three Rivers Press, 2005.

Lewisohn, Mark. *The Complete Beatles Recording Sessions*. London: Hamlyn Press, 2004.

Lewisohn, Mark. *Tune In, The Beatles All These Years*. New York: Crown Archetype, 2013.

Martin, George. *All You Need Is Ears*. New York: St. Martin's Press, 1979.

Miles, Barry. *Many Years From Now*. New York: Henry Holt and Company, Inc., 1997.

Norman, Philip. *John Lennon, The Life*. New York: HarperCollins, 2008.

O'Tool, Kit. *Beatlefan Magazine*. Issue 233, July/August 2018.

Porter, Richard. *Guide to Beatles*. London: England. Fab Four Enterprises, 2000.

Howard, Ron. Imagine Entertainment. *Eight Days A Week: The Touring Years,* 2016.

Shankar, Ravi. *My Music, My Life*. San Rafael, CA: Mandala Books, 2007.

Sounes, Howard. *Fab: An Intimate Life of Paul McCartney*. Cambridge: De Capo Press, 2010.

Spitz, Bob. *The Beatles*. New York: Back Bay Books, 2000.

Taylor, Alistair. *A Secret History*. London: John Blake Publishing, 2001.

TheBeatlesBible.com and *Wikipeda.com* for the Beatles Discography.

Thompson, Gordon. *Please Please Me*. New York: Oxford University Press, Inc., 2008.

Tingen, Paul. *Sound On Sound Magazine*. Volume 32, August 2017.

Turner, Steve. *A Hard Day's Write*. United Kingdom: Carlton Books Limited, 1994.

Value of Persistence. Lucas and Nordgren. Journal of Personality/ Social Psychology #109, 2015.

PHOTOGRAPHY CREDITS

Photographs of Mitch Murray courtesy of Mitch Murray, 2016.

"Love Me Do" Tollie Records 45rpm sleeve and publicity photo of Beatles circa 1963, courtesy of American Pie Records, Ventura, CA.

Photo of George Harrison with Jackie Lomax courtesy of Jackie Lomax in 2013.